I0503895

How to Get a Job in an Office in 30 Days

By Winning the Interview Game!

A step by step game plan for school, college and university graduates.

By Ex CEO, and Employment Coach
Jason Hogan

Published by Maldek House © 2016-2018 All Rights Reserved
Revised Edition 2018

Printed by CreateSpace

ISBN-13: 978-1717088543

ISBN-10: 1717088546

In Association with

www.EziEnglish.com

Also available as an ebook

Dedicated to everyone I have ever helped to get a job in the past, and to all the people who have given me jobs when I needed them.

Thank you.

Disclaimer

This book is just a guide and is meant to supplement, not replace, your knowledge and experience. Every interview is different. Circumstances will vary. Past experiences given as examples may no longer be relevant due to changing or differing laws.

The author and publisher take no responsibility for any problems that may incur as a result of using the information in this book. Although the author and publisher have made every effort to ensure that the information in this book was correct at press time, the author and publisher do not assume and hereby disclaim any liability to any party for any loss, damage, or disruption caused by errors or omissions, whether such errors or omissions result from negligence, accident, or any other cause. Always consult a qualified professional before following the advice in this book, as individual circumstances will affect the outcome.

Examples use fictional characters. Any similarities to people living or dead are completely coincidental.

No attempt is made to supersede any trademarks. Any references to businesses are positive, but are not official endorsements. All mention of business names in this book are for review and illustration purposes only and have been capitalized to show respect for their copyrights.

Contents

Introduction

Thank you for making the intention to actively find a job, and grab this title as one of many things to help you.

This book is for recent school leavers, college and university graduates, and anyone who is applying for an office job for the first time.

This book assumes you have, at the very least, senior high school skills and a good command of the English language.

The book also focuses more on office type jobs (the easiest to get and keep) rather than other types of work like retail, construction or freelance work which are likely to be short term, though many of the techniques in the book can be applied to these areas.

It also assumes you have excellent verbal and written communication skills.

If your written and spoken language is not up to scratch, then I recommend doing a literacy course. If English is your second language, and you believe it is holding you back, you should fix this first asap. You can find an online tutor on www.TutorAgent.com

Keep the following in the forefront of your mind whenever you're looking for a job and attending an interview, as it will help you have the right mindset when offering your services.

1. The business wants to find someone who will make it more money and solve their problems.

2. The business wants someone who won't cost it much money or cause them problems.

3. The business wants someone who will work hard, continuously and in a focused way without being distracted, or causing distraction for other employees.

4. The business wants an employee who always arrives early, leaves late, doesn't spend too much time on toilet breaks, lunch breaks or smoking breaks.

5. The business wants an employee who actively makes a passionate contribution to the future of the business, and cares about the business like it

was their own child, sacrificing their life and family for the betterment of the business.

6. The business wants someone who will fit the culture and customs of its workplace and is unlikely to object, based on personal preferences, to how things are done within the business.

7. The business needs a product or tool (you) that will be useful, and it will keep it for as long as that product or tool is useful. If the product or tool stops being useful, or the business changes and the product or tool's function is no longer relevant, then the business will suffer as a result and it will need to find a new product or tool to keep being able to make money, if the product or tool cannot be upgraded to fit.

8. The business wants someone with common sense who can think outside the box, plan far ahead, and always avoid future problems

Whenever you look for a job, also keep this in mind "How can I help this business make money?" When you're in the interview, think about "I want to help this business to be successful." When you're working at your new job think "I want to do everything possible to make sure this business is a success now and into the future."

If you're okay with that, you're ready to begin looking for an office job.

Good luck!

Jason

P.S. Finding a job is a very stressful and serious business, so I've written this book in a gaming style to help reduce the anxiety where possible. Whether you find it fun, or groan at my attempt, I'm hoping it'll put you in a lighter mood to tackle this area of your life. As you work through the sections of the interview game plan, note your points and work hard to level up! If you keep a positive mindset about searching for work, and see it as more of a game, than some seriously terrible life changing situation, you increase your ability to find a job!

How to Get a Job in an Office in 30 Days
By Winning the Interview Game!

Beginner Level

Level 1 – Pre-Preparation

Win the Positive Mindset Game

Before you even start writing your resume, you need to change your mindset.

If you're down because you don't have money, stressed because you don't have money, worried about all the bills because you don't have money, then the smell of sweat and fear is going to be emanating from you all the time and people will avoid you. Yes, they will! You'll constantly be losing points, until you're down to zero.

Start thinking about all the positive things in your life. Walk in the park. Ring an old friend and talk about the fun times (don't mention your money problems) Get your positive points back up. Live in the now, and don't dwell on the past or worry about the far future.

When you put more focus on your lack of money, or lack of a job you change your whole physical persona. Stressed, anxious, depressed people are usually bent over, frowning, talking about their stress with everyone they meet.

You don't want to be like that. Contact people who are bubbly and fun. Copy their behavior. Get excited by cute things. Get that energy level up, and keep it there. Not an act, you really need to change yourself inside to be happy.

Now, when you're happy, what happens? Your face is calm, smiling slightly. Your head is up, your shoulders back, you lose your stoop, you walk purposefully, confidently, you discerningly smile more at people. Everything becomes positive. You start to see positive things in the world around you.

If something negative happens, you know it is already in the past and you've moved on. You stay happy in all situations, seeing everything as neutral.

Being happy doesn't just improve your job prospects, it improves your relationship prospects, too. It also improves your service at restaurants. Everyone loves happy people and they'll do their best to bring more happiness out of happy people. They won't bother with sad, depressed, complaining, angry, stressed people as that is too much work. Don't make too much work for other people. Being positive is key to getting everything you want in life.

So, throw away those complaints, forget your problems, don't listen to others' problems, keep yourself positive, and work on continuing to increase your positivity level.

But, I'm sure you're saying "That's not right. I should be upset about this situation. I should listen to that sad person. I should be down because that's the right way to behave."

Who told you that?

It's a social construct. It's a simple mindset you can break. Most successful people are positive people, no matter what the situation!

And, I'm sorry for being direct about it but, being sad about any situation isn't going to pay your bills. If someone wants to drag you into their negativity you just have to say no, and go somewhere else to be positive. So, the absolute start of your journey to getting a job or your next job is positivity.

Goal 150+ points of positivity today!
Weekly goal of 1000+ points

Positivity and Negativity

Let's take a closer look at positivity and negativity in relation to getting that job.

Do you know how many negative people have come to me complaining that the world owes them and they don't know why they aren't getting a job?

These are usually the same people that can't keep a relationship or can't hold onto friends or can't hold a job once they get one.

If you're toxic, potential employers will know this straight away.

Toxic people complain all the time, think that the world should give them something because of something they did in the past. They expect everything to be easy because they deserve it.

Or they've been on the pension for years, used community services all the time, or just think that the government's responsibility is to take care of them, not take care of themselves.

They have a me, me, me mindset.

Now, it may not be through any fault of their own. After all, as children we ALL have the me, me, me mindset. It's a protection mechanism while we're vulnerable, and it encourages older people around us to want to help us. But as we get older we're supposed to get rid of that mindset, and move our focus outward, to helping those younger and more vulnerable than us to succeed.

The problem is that there are some people who never move beyond the extreme selfish, childish nature and turn to the government to be their surrogate parents when they're adults. These are the hardest people to change the mindset of. If you are starting to think like that, you'll spiral into a negative mindset very quickly. No government can be the perfect parent to all people, so you're going to be disappointed. Trust in yourself and you'll be more positive.

The fact that you're reading this book suggests you don't have this mindset. If you did, you probably wouldn't be reading it. 30 Days? Too long!

But it is important to mention, as you may accidentally give this impression in the interview, and the employer may think you're a toxic, negative person. This is the number one reason for your resume being shifted to the round file. Employers will not hire people they think will either cause problems for their business or problems for other staff members down the track. Smiling, laughing, confident, happy, cheerful, joyful, loving, caring people are more likely to get the job.

People who have negative mindsets or negative traits usually also attract people with the same mindsets and traits to them. So, even if a person decides that they won't be negative anymore, all their friends and relatives will quickly bring them back down again. Perhaps the only way a negative person can change is if they completely distance themselves from every negative person in their life. That means dropping all negative friends, and moving out of a negative home, or getting a divorce from a negative relationship, if necessary, to avoid a toxic family.

If you're in a negative situation at home, or all your friends are negative, even if you try and fake it, those nagging doubts are going to surface on your face and the employer will know straight away that there is a potential bomb in the chair opposite that he or she doesn't want to bring into the business.

Tattoos/piercings/messy hair/swear words/slang/poor English = negative/toxic person

In the old days, employers would simply look at a tattoo and decide that that person was too negative for his business. Now, in most western countries, tattoos are cool and there are many amazingly positive people with them, (even people who can land spaceships on comets!), but old employers still have the same mindset so they expect a person with a tattoo to be negative.

Also, employers would listen for swear words or slang and decide that person was too confrontational, or would cause too many conflicts in the workplace. Now, it isn't so much of a problem in the 21st century as most western country work places are multicultural, and the meaning of a swear word or negative slang word may not be understood by most professionals. But old employers still have the same mindset so they expect a person who swears or uses slang to be negative.

So, the trick is to make sure you are not only positive in your voice but positive in your outlook on life. Having a fear of no money coming in will give the employer the impression you're negative. So, go in positively. And how do you feel positive when you're feeling down about no money? Make sure you don't have time to think about it! Schedule at least 5 interviews a week, send out lots of resumes, make calls, go for walks in the park, be active, be positive, and most of all, think happy thoughts.

(Of course, if you have tattoos or piercings, if you believe the employer you want to apply with is going to object to tattoos, piercings, and other things, then either it isn't the sort of job you should be doing, or it's a job you'll need to change yourself for.)

If you keep your happy, positive outlook going for at least two weeks the world will look brighter, the job interviews more fun, and you're more than likely to get a job within 30 days.

Things to do to change your brain chemistry to be more positive:

Stop drinking alcohol! (10 points)
I love wine. I've even made a small YouTube channel devoted to it - www.youtube.com/user/prizewines I love nothing better to type away while drinking a thick and juicy shiraz or cabernet sauvignon. However, too much alcohol for too long changes brain chemistry, reducing your positivity

level. It increases your inability to inhibit negative impulses and emotions. Just don't have any until you have been in your new job for at least six months. Many alcoholics are very negative, angry people, prone to short tempers and fighting. This is the effect of excess alcohol on the brain suppressing dopamine and oxytocin, your happiness hormones. Give it up for at least six months and see what happens.

Stop eating/drinking sugar! (10 points)
This is another thing that causes major fluctuations in brain chemistry and causes depression, sleeping disorders and more. Everything contains sugar these days, so avoiding sugar may mean going vegan! See what you can do about not eating anything with sugar in it. Check the ingredients on every packet before you buy them and even if you must have it, make sure sugar is listed as the last of the ingredients (meaning it is a really small amount) rather than near the top of the list of ingredients (meaning it is a really large amount.)

Reduce daily caffeine intake (10 points)
1-2 cups of coffee or tea a day is enough. (Check caffeinated drinks like energy drinks and sports drinks) No caffeine after 3pm. Enough to keep the neurons firing but not enough to cause sleepless nights which will also result in depression and negativity. Many students have been on 5 or 6 cups of coffee or bottles of energy drinks for years. You need to reduce your intake, and start repairing your body. Initially you'll get headaches from withdrawal symptoms, so start reducing as soon as possible, before your first interview.

Increase your uninterrupted sleep period (10 points)
Minimum 7-8 hours a day. Sleep will refresh your body and mind and keep negative thoughts away. It will also help you have a clear mind for the interview. You need a week of at least 7-8 hours uninterrupted sleep to get your brain regenerated. Alcohol, caffeine, noise and bright lights disturb your normal sleep cycle, so you might still feel tired after even ten hours' sleep.

A regular sleep cycle can also help. Constantly changing sleep times will disrupt the internal rhythms of the body. Sleep 11pm to 6am or 12pm to 7am. Keep the cycle. If you can't keep a regular sleep cycle it will increase your negativity.

Put away the screens (10 points)
Stop looking at any kind of screen, including your mobile, by 10pm every night (preferably by 8pm every night). Bright light and screens keep you awake and disrupt your sleeping patterns. Make an intention to turn everything off by 10pm and get ready for bed.

Avoid the news (unless you need it for your job) (10 points)

Don't watch the news or read newspapers, unless you are following a specific market, or industry, and then only read those sections. Avoid all negative news. Negative news will get you depressed about the world and subtly change your outlook in an interview.

Avoid/Unfriend/Disassociate/Remove toxic, negative people from your life (20 points)

Avoid all your toxic relatives, friends and acquaintances, until you're secure in your job. If you have a particularly needy friend that's always calling you to complain about something, tell them that you're working on an important project and can't speak with them for a month. If you live with negative, toxic people, find a place away from them while they're awake. Do your preparation in a library or a café or a park, somewhere away from things that will get you down.

Meditation (20 points)

This may not be for everyone but many advocates of mindfulness recommend that you start meditating. Listen to some meditation recordings or simply sit by yourself somewhere calm and peaceful and think happy thoughts.

Get some music or guided meditation files to help you get into the right state. Most of the time we are in what doctors call a beta state. Most happy and positive people are in an alpha state - a state just below the beta state.

Unfortunately, you need the beta state to work in an office, so meditate to the alpha state to refresh yourself, then bring yourself back to a more positive beta. This mix of brain activity will enable you to have both an alpha rhythm and a beta rhythm while working, increasing your positivity.

Put aside time to pursue personal goals and passions (20 points)

Do things that are positive for you. Things that you enjoy. Put aside time for them to get your happiness level up. Before you start writing your resumes, cover letters and preparing for interviews, you need a happy mindset so that your writing sounds happy too. Make sure you're feeling positive when you apply for jobs. Follow your passion, joys and things that excite you so that you're in a good frame of mind all the time.

Plan happy dreams (20 points)

Go to sleep with the intention of having happy dreams. Start the dream of having a conversation with happy people and let it take you from there. Do this every night until it becomes a habit. You could also write in detail what you'd like to experience in your dream and then read it back to yourself before you go to sleep. (Write in pencil on paper. Don't use a pc or any other screen)

Set a deep, passionate intention of getting a job within 30 days (50 points)

Set an intention to get a job within 30 days. Write this down everywhere. Make it your login on your computer. Be thinking about it in a positive way. Not 'I need a job in 30 days because I don't have money' (negative) but 'I'll get a job within 30 days and it'll be easy' (positive!) Put positive pictures and things around this statement so that you feel happy when you see it.

Whatever happens in the world, smile, and stay positive. If you've been negative for a long time, it might take time for your body to get rid of the toxins it has created and stored as a result. (Negative people get sick, a lot!) You might even find yourself crying to release them. Do it, and be happy.

Outside the box (Analyze yourself) (30 points per solution)

If you've done everything above, and still don't feel a bit happier by the end of the week, you may be affected by other things in your environment. There are thousands of possibilities, from the fumes of fire retardant on furniture to the flickering of fluorescent lighting. Everyone can be affected differently, depending on how their DNA has evolved to suit the particular environment they're in.

There are other things people can do to be happy that are more specific to individuals, like avoiding dairy and gluten to reduce IBS, or moving to a place less noisy so that you have uninterrupted sleep. Or moving extension cords in your apartment so that the buzz of electromagnetic radiation and the heat of Wi-Fi doesn't disturb your sleep either. Even replacing mercury fillings in your teeth with a non-mercury composite, or wearing socks all the time, can help some sensitive individuals. But you will know what these are and how to fix them to give you a happier disposition.

So, the summary of all this - that you need to rewire your brain to be positive. Act positive, think positive 24/7 and you'll soon get a job. Employers will be beating down your door to get a happy person to work for them.

If you've succeeded in becoming a positive person, that job is now a lot closer.

Level Up!

Level 2

Remove Cognitive Distortions
and Change Life Habits

Cognitive Distortions

Every human suffers from these, no exceptions. A cognitive distortion is an incorrect thought that has been reinforced, either by others telling you it is correct, or a few negative experiences you've had when you were younger that your mind is saying applies to all experiences. It's our ego's way of protecting us. Sometimes you just need to tell your ego to mind its own business, and get on with being positive.

There are millions, so I'd advise searching the net for 'cognitive distortions' and reading the hundreds of psychology reports and commentary on the subject.

No time for that? Okay, there are three that you need to know now.

1. A propensity to jump to conclusions
This is when, just by reading someone's reaction, you decide they're thinking something specific, either a negative thought about the world or a negative thought about you.

You actually don't know what they're thinking, but your ego says 'oh, they're thinking bad thoughts about me. This is terrible,' when the actual situation may be that the person has just eaten something that disagreed with them and it is showing on their face.

While intuition can be good when the messages seem mixed, when you've already decided 100 percent what their body language means, it is more than likely not your intuition. Don't jump to conclusions. Always ask, or think positively, and give them the benefit of the doubt.

2. A belief that fairness exists and everything should be rewarded
People believe that with their experience, their abilities, their effort, their time, their hard work, their contribution etc., that they must get something in exchange for this. That the world around them owes them something specific. That, because they did something, they deserve something back.

Unfortunately, the world has proved time and again that it doesn't work like that. We have a very unusual idea of what 'fair' is. Life is not always 'fair'. If you go through life judging fairness in everything, based on give and take, you'll always be disappointed because your idea of fairness is completely different to how the world works.

Ask all the people who spent their lives caring for those in charity situations only to end up in the same situation at the end of their lives.

Or those that spent their lives partying and making thousands of friends only to die alone in a hospital.

Or those that put their life and soul into a business only to see the world move on and decide that the service they'd put their thirty years of life into is no longer relevant or needed in society today. If you allow this idea of 'life should be fair' get to you and control you, you're always going to be disappointed. It is a thought process you need to get rid of.

However, there is another type of fairness that modern society seems to have forgotten. The gift of life. The gift of beauty in the everyday. The air we breathe, the colors of nature, the existence of others, and a lot more.

If you give gratitude simply for being alive, and give thanks that the planet can support you, then life is already infinitely fairer than you could ever dream, and you could spend your entire life making up for it!

If you exist, if you are reading this, you've already won, and everything you have and can do is already a bonus.

In this sense, the only way for life to be unfair is if someone was to go back in time and stop you from existing. Otherwise, when you die, then everything is equal, not unfair.

Find a way to view the world other than fair and unfair, and you'll be a much more positive person.

3. Shoulds
People should behave this way. People should do that. People shouldn't be doing that. This is a set of rules we've been brought up to believe, and we think that this is how the world works. Simply travelling overseas shows us quickly that other cultures don't have the same 'shoulds' that we do.

If you find someone behaving a different way to how you think they should behave...

If you feel anger, resentment, frustration or guilt because of a situation that has happened, as you believe it should have gone another way…

If you feel that your ten years of experience mean that someone should employ you over someone with only two years of experience…

These thoughts hold us in negative patterns and don't let us move forward.

What can you do?
Make a list of your beliefs, and see if there are any that are part of cognitive distortions lists, and work on getting rid of them. Sorting these out quickly will mean reaching that happiness point a lot sooner.

When you have zero expectations about getting the job, paradoxically, you've got a better chance of getting the job!

For each cognitive distortion you find and overcome, add 20 points.

Change Life Habits

One of the things I've noticed about many people is that they seem to get stuck in a rut very quickly. Not a slow downward progression into a hole that they struggle in for a while and then get out of again, but a sudden slip into repetitive behavior without any conscious regard to how stuck they've suddenly become. A habit that suddenly can't be broken.

Like saying the same thing several times in a conversation.

Or holding a thought about how angry they are of a situation and mentioning it again the next day or week or even a month later.

Some habits they may have formed in childhood, thought they were acceptable then, and now can't understand how their social fun is not acceptable in the workplace (like farting and laughing, or using f***ing as an adjective for everything.)

There are lessons we need to learn in life to help us grow, but holding onto any kind of past situation means it is so much harder to move to the future.

It's like dragging a one hundred kilo bag around with you. What seems to be a positive thing actually weighs you down.

Writers don't keep promoting the same book they wrote years ago.

Actors don't keep talking about the same movie they were in years ago.

Scientists don't keep going over their own research from years ago.

Musicians don't keep promoting the song that was a number 1 hit years ago.

You need to do this in your life and let go of things that hold you back. As one of my mentors once said, 'You can't move forward by patting yourself on the back.'

Then there are the negative habits.

That friend that insists on drinking every Friday night who'll get upset if you don't.

That parent who rings you and cries on the phone for hours all the time, that you can't hang up on.

That child that keeps taking your attention away from you when they could simply learn to play by themselves (or you could put them into a day care center for while)

I knew a friendly, kind, caring, considerate guy in his early fifties. Hardworking, conscientious, did anything for people. Used to be a bus driver, so he received the worst behavior from people, but still stayed positive.

His one fault was that he loved making sexist jokes. Loved it like it was the only thing he could talk about.

I felt uncomfortable on behalf of my work colleagues because of this person's behavior, but most of the people in the office didn't understand his jokes, as they spoke English as a second language.

Even so, it wasn't acceptable, and I tried to reign in his behavior without success. It was ingrained in him that the way to make male friends was to make sexist jokes.

This was true up until the 70s in most western countries. People have grown since then, the world has changed, but old habits from old traditions and previous generations still exist.

If you grew up with that habit, and the world changed around you to say that it was no longer acceptable, do you change with the world or rail against it?

If you decide to fight the world, say the world is now wrong, that everyone has been conditioned a certain way, that everyone is too PC, and you'll have none of that, then you're set in your ways, and getting a job is going to become almost impossible for you.

Change is a part of life. Everything changes. All the time. You need to go with the flow and change yourself to fit.

As far as I know, he went back to driving buses in the CBD a few years ago. An easy job to get as no one wants the constant insults, or cleaning the bus at the end of the day. If he had updated his personality and behavior, he might have been able to get and keep something that pays better. (Not that there's anything wrong with driving a bus!)

If you have already recognized you had a habit that was acceptable years ago, but not now, and you have already got rid of that habit, add 20 points. If you find others that you still have and you get rid of them now, add 50 points per habit.

Breaking the Negative Thinking Cycle

If you usually think negatively about something that didn't go your way, that is also another habit. Just say 'Oh, well, maybe next time' and move on.

"Oh, well, maybe next time"

I didn't get the job. Oh, well, maybe next time.

I missed the train. Oh, well, there'll be another one.

I didn't get the date. Oh, well. Plenty of fish in the sea.

I missed out on the last sushi roll. Oh, well. There are other stores, other days.

The concert was sold out. Oh, well. There are other things in life.

I couldn't make the party. Oh, well. There'll be other parties.

**Other things that may cause you to feel negativity,
that you need may need to work on:**

Anxious about interviews because of your race?

In some countries, racism plays a big part in the way people think. Not because it happens, but because people apply it to every situation, believing that is the only reason. If you keep thinking racism is the reason, then you won't be able to see what the real reason is.

If you didn't get the job and you have a habit of thinking 'Oh I didn't get it because I wasn't white, and it's all about white supremacy' or 'this place has no Asians so I think they just don't like Asians' then you aren't expanding your thinking to look at other reasons you might not have got the job.

If you then dwell on this, and think about chasing that 'racist' business or talking about it with others, you're stopping your thinking from moving forward, and you're stopping yourself finding a place where you would be better suited to work.

Of course, this is quite common thinking for school leavers, and even those in college who haven't had much experience working in different offices. But once you've had a few jobs, you'll find that most businesses are quite professional, as it is what a person can do, not where they come from, that is important.

In my experience, where someone comes from has never ever been a factor in me hiring them for a job, nor has it been a factor in many of the businesses I've worked as a colleague. Many businesses are equal opportunity employers and advertise as such. If you suspect one really isn't, then it's best to avoid that business, and go for a job at another place instead. This is one of the reasons we always spend a little bit of extra time researching the company first before applying.

Many businesses have LinkedIn and Facebook pages, as well as reviews on job-seeking sites. If a company really is racist, you'll easily be able to find this out long before sending them a resume.

Anxious about interviews because of your weight?

In some places, your weight may be a factor. Many small restaurants don't have enough space between the chairs, or in their tiny kitchens, for a large waiter or waitress to fit, so the business usually only hire short, thin staff. (Think max 110 pounds / 50kg) Airlines use a Body Mass Index to calculate weight. If you're outside what's expected, apply when you've lost enough weight, or apply for a different job.

If you have weight problems, there are jobs out there better suited to you. If you go to one of those interviews and discover it isn't for you, it's an 'oh well' moment. Move on to the next interview, rather than be angry at the business for not considering bigger people.

Anxious about interviews because of your age?

Perhaps you're already over fifty? Unless you're still working out at the gym or doing yoga three times a week, then any employer is going to be concerned about his insurance, your ability to work fast, and whether you're able to be trained, purely because there are way too many 'old' people in the world saying 'Oh, I'm too old to learn new tricks.'

The assumption we make is you can't. I've hired older people before who say they can learn anything, then I've put them in front of a computer and they spend the whole day trying to work out how to type an email that should have been sent in one minute. Now I test everyone in interviews. If they can't multitask with three computers, several interdepartmental message popups, a call and a call waiting, as well as someone coming in to ask them a question, then they won't cope in my office.

When I took a job at a wine company, they were downsizing, and needed someone like me to deal with one call center position and one membership management position. Being a fast worker, I did both positions for two years, saving them employing a second person. I was in my 40s at the time and worked harder than some of the staff in their twenties in one position.

Interestingly, there were many older people in their fifties and sixties who worked harder than I did. So, there is no such thing as ageism, only skills and ability. If you stay fit, active, keep up-to-date on the latest technology and are a fast worker, age should not hold you back. Especially as you'll usually be able to prove it in an interview test!

In city areas, employers are now checking resumes to see if you have studied anything in the past few months. They're more likely to hire someone who is still studying, or has just recently completed a course on something. So, age is not a factor as you can study something at any age. Take up a new business-related course and start looking for jobs. Employers love people still focused on improving themselves, no matter what their age is.

Too Young and Inexperienced?

Too inexperienced? Employers love sponges. Straight from uni, easy to be molded to the corporate way of thinking. You might even have been head hunted before you finished your studies.

Keep trying. Lots of 'oh well' moments for you. Learn a new skill while you're looking for that job, or take on part-time jobs as you travel around the world.

You could also do some volunteer work as an intern and get valuable experience.

If you don't get the job straight away, don't get upset because you spent all that money on resume printing, taxi rides and renting that suit. Keep trying! Most employment books, websites and coaches are there to help people in their twenties. If you're driven to succeed, you should have the least amount of problems of any job seekers.

For each anxiety you overcome, add 50 points.

--

If you have fixed all your cognitive distortions, broken all your old habits, or at the very least have accepted them and can move on from them. Add 2000 points and
Level up!

Level 3
Stabilizing Your Emotions

Emotional Quotient (EQ)

Once you have become an extremely positive person, and have a better outlook on life after removing your cognitive distortions, your emotions should have stabilized. You're more likely to react positively to a negative situation. You'll hardly feel frustrated or get angry at anything. Tears will be a thing of the past, or something you'll do rarely. You'll have a consistently calm demeanor.

Employers will not employ someone who is likely to get angry about anything. If you act angry about something in the interview, even if it is just a slight flicker of emotion on your face, the employer will know. In fact, we test these things all the time. We might set an interview time then make you wait twenty minutes. Tell you the interview time has changed and could you come another time, or call you at inconvenient times for phone interviews. It's just to see how you'll react.

When I was running my ESL college I would take teachers to the pub, buy them drinks, and see how they reacted to my interview once they were a bit tipsy. As an Australian, drinking is a very strong part of my culture and heritage (there's a pub on every corner!) and the job required them to attend a pub meeting with students on a Friday night. My teachers had to be able to drink, handle their drink, and keep calm in the face of possible stressful situations. It was an easy way for me to weed out the good from the best. I only ever hired extremely calm people, or people who could confront me on issues in a calm and polite way, and those people were usually those who could handle their drinks well. (And, if they had an RSA – Responsible Service of Alcohol certificate – even better!)

If you have extreme problems with your emotions. Sad one minute, angry the next, easily stressed or frustrated, you have other problems you need to fix. Start doing meditation every morning for an hour to get your mind under control. If that doesn't work, please see a counsellor or psychologist for some therapy. It will make getting that job, and keeping it, much easier.

If you'd like to take this idea of emotional control to a higher level, I recommend researching Neuro-linguistic Programming. (NLP)

For each emotion you get under control, add 500 points. If you are in complete control of all your emotions, add 2000 points and
Level up!

Level 4
Prioritize Money
(from a positive perspective!)

Prioritizing Money is not about Discounts!

This may seem like a no brainer but, most people don't prioritize money. You might be thinking 'I save, I look for discounts, I only spend on what I need, I always look for the best price on something,' then you've already proven you don't prioritize money. Prioritizing money isn't about the money, it's about the value.

How much is a minute in a day worth to you?

If you spent two hours shopping around to save $5 on a pair of shoes, you've already spent $5 more on those shoes! Not to mention the wear and tear on the car you used, the petrol you spent, the soles of the shoes you're wearing, the time you spent worrying about saving which could affect your health in the long run, as well as whatever you spent on snacks and drinks while looking around for ways to save. You might have spent $50 to save $5.

What could you have done in those two hours that could have made you money? What things could you be involved in that will result in a payoff later?

Successful business people always look at the value of time, and do things like pay someone else to do something better than they can. (That's one of the reasons why they want to hire you.) Which is better? The business person spending 100 hours of his time trying to work out the next Photoshop update so that he can create a new image for his mobile app, or hiring a student for $15 per hour who can do it in 10 hours, initially costing him $150, but saving him 100 hours of his time?

Every second is worth money. Every single second. Shorten your showers, your time spent in the bathroom, the time you spend reading news reports, playing games, playing Pokémon Go, talking with friends, watching sport, shopping for clothes.

What about those times you spend in the pub drinking, that then translates to lost time the next day recovering from a hangover? Did you spend $100 on drinks or $500 on lost time?

As soon as you start to see that every second counts and that you can make a difference in your life by making sure not a second is wasted, you'll soon be able to think like the business that wants you to work for them.

When you prioritize the financial value of your time over all else, that job is going to show up quickly. You'll have the mindset that says 'The only thing that is important is getting that job. I will not stop until I have that job that I want. Nothing will stand in my way. I will get that job.'

Employers are looking for that sign of commitment to show through your behavior. They'll quickly see the difference between someone who just wants to get a job to pay their bills, and someone who is focused on earning the money. There is a whole different demeanor. Sitting up straight in the chair, having perfectly cut hair, perfectly cared for clothes, a sense of focus.

If you attend an interview, and you slouch in your chair, your shirt isn't tucked in, your hair hasn't been cut in weeks, and your eyes flick around the room being easily distracted by everything, then the employer knows you'll be hard to 'fix' and won't consider you for the job he or she wants.

If you're focused, answer everything quickly, succinctly, with no pauses, have a positive and money-oriented attitude, ask about profits and potential for future business, can discuss money matters, your chance of getting a job improves.

Research Game!

Still not sure what I'm talking about? Try this exercise:

Create a spreadsheet with five columns.

Write down the numbers 1 to 24 in a column. These will be your hours in the day.

Next to these write down what you did in these hours.

Next to these, assign a monetary value. So, watching something on your TV or computer will be $0.00, for example. Going to the toilet, but spending longer than you need to as you're posting on Facebook and Instagram, or creating memes, would also be $0.00.

Next to these, assign a usage cost – how much you spent to do that activity. (So, watching TV would be -$1.00 per hour for electricity and wear and tear on the carpet lounge and television. Take more off if you ate during it. Sitting on a toilet uses electricity, the power you used to charge the phone and the power that run the light bulb in your bathroom. So, maybe $0.50)

In the fifth column, make a mark next to the ones you believe were completely unnecessary and were a waste of your time. If you're not sure, think about whether doing that today will have any relevance to your life within the next ten years. So, obviously watching television won't have any relevance in your life in 2028, unless it was a documentary on a career you'd like to take up in the future.

At the bottom, add up the hours spent on the ones you thought were completely unnecessary.

Let's say, for the day, you get 12 wasted hours.

I judge my minimum time as $1 per minute, so $60 per hour. That is just me and it is just for ease of calculation. I use it as my reminder to always be focused on making money. In Sydney, Australia, that is a low salary. Many people earn a lot more than that. However, allowing for exchange rates and rates of pay in your area, perhaps you could start by calculating $0.10 per minute, so $6.00 an hour. $72.00 for 12 hours. Did you waste $72.00 plus expenses today?

This exercise is just to give you an idea of what you are spending.

So, rather than watching something, or doing other things that don't make money, why not find a job that pays $6.00 an hour to start, while you're looking for something better, and fill in those non-money-making times with some much-needed cash?

Do you see how you can quickly get yourself out of the rut of not having any money? Of not having a job? Do you see how a simple mindset change will enable you to earn more, while looking for that even better job?

How many hours a week are currently wasted that you could be putting to good use and making money from?

If you're serious about money, you'll be able to consider leaving your family and friends and relocating too!

Military officers, government officials, doctors, seafarers, oil refinery workers, miners and more do it all the time. Millions move interstate and overseas every day to take up work. If the money is important, you need to consider leaving your family and friends behind and travelling to get that job. Or taking them with you to another country if your partner agrees. That opens up a whole world of possibilities for you.

The takeaway for a successful life is to prioritize money.

Having said that, that is something for people in their 20s and 30s. I'm in my 40s and no longer prioritize money. I'm happy with my PC, my tiny rented studio apartment, and a bottle of wine a week. But, when I was in my thirties it was all I could think about, due to family and friends pushing me to keep earning. If you want to earn money, get an office job and keep the money mindset. Once you're over that, relax and enjoy your life!

Prioritize money.

If you have been able to change your mindset to prioritize money, you can

Level up! (2000 points)

Level 5
Update Your Work Ethic

Work Harder!

So, now that you have changed yourself to be more positive, and changed your behavior to be more focused and active, it's time to look at your general work ethic.

How hard do you work?

Here are some traits most employers look for in an employee.

Do you have these traits?

Expected Employee Traits

1. Never complain

2. Take on a project without questioning why

3. Do everything fast

4. Do everything efficiently

5. Always ask if directions are unclear

6. Always get feedback on their work, and receive the feedback positively (even if negative)

7. Push harder to get things done by thinking outside the box where possible

8. Utilize colleagues, friends and relatives for advice on complicated projects so that the job is done in half the time. (While retaining confidentiality.)

9. Have a propensity to come in early, skip all breaks including lunch, and leave late, to make sure the job is done. (Of course, nice managers always insist that you go on your breaks, even if you don't want to. A lot of managers don't notice.)

10. Rarely make any mistakes, and mistakes, if they do occur, are corrected quickly.

11. Extreme attention to detail, even surpassing the manager's perfectionist nature.

12. Happy to work on the lowest legal pay, or as a free intern in return for training.

13. Usually, no training needed.

14. Will take home work and work over the weekend and bring completed work in on Monday without being requested to, not telling the manager about it and completing the project in record time. (Of course, nice managers, when they find out, sometimes can give a bonus.)

15. Be open to working 16 hours a day, 7 days a week on rotating shifts, or on call.

--

So, that's what a lot of employers want.

They want someone hardworking like that.

Someone who is not distracted by family, friends, parties, alcohol, and other things that may reduce that person's performance in the work environment.

Someone who is available 24/7 and only has their mind for the job.

Are you about to say, "It **should**n't be like that!"?

Of course, there are government and community rules in place that businesses should follow.

Of course, people need holidays, people should only work a certain number of hours a week etc. etc.

Tell that to nurses, doctors, paramedics and surgeons who work 100 hours per week, people who work in retail stores during the holiday season, CEOs who need to work seven days to keep their business profitable so that they can pay their staff, and more.

Most businesses in the world want workers with this kind of work ethic. If you go to an interview with a resume that suggests you have this kind of work ethic, the business will pay more attention to you than to a person who obviously doesn't.

Now, the quickest way to get into this kind of mindset is start doing it at home. Clean your home, do the shopping, start renovating, find a project and work your guts out on it. Take on some volunteer work and practice working hard. You'll quickly understand the hard work habit and can show that in a job interview. The employer will smell it on you!

Have you been working at something 100 hours a week?

Have you got the work mindset?

Level up (2000 points)

Ding Ding. Congratulations!

Positive Mindset – Tick

Cognitive Distortions Removed and Habits Broken – Tick

Emotions Stabilized - Tick

Money Prioritized – Tick

Strong Work Ethic Implemented – Tick

You've attained the skill of

'Competent'!

You are now at the

Intermediate Level

Intermediate Level

Level 6: Perceptions

It's time to collect your tools and level up again.

**Perception Tool,
Advertising Tool A,
Advertising Tool B,
Communication Tool A,
Communication Tool B**

After collecting your tools, you can then send resumes and cover letters
For every resume and cover letter you send, add 20 points.
For every phone interview 50 points
For every in-person job interview 100 points
For every second in-person job interview 200 points

Your goal is to reach 7,500 points within 21 days.

Perception Tool: You are a product!

You need to think of yourself as a product that needs to be constantly updated and upgraded to fit today's society.

You need to continuously be working on improving yourself.

Only stop for a few moments on one day a week for a break.

Imagine every hour you're not working can be put into doing something productive to improve 'you' for your next stage of work.

The better the product, the more versatile it is, the more that people want to buy it. Prepare yourself to be the best product that everyone wants, and businesses will be knocking down your door to hire you.

But don't wait for them. If you have a passion for something, you can go door knocking, send out letters, emails, speak with people, go to groups, network, and sell yourself to everyone you meet.

Create business cards, and hand them out.

Make flyers of yourself, and post them.

You want to sell yourself like a product so that people will want to buy you.

Many of you know this already. This is selling yourself 101 and we quickly learn this in school.

Doing any kind of job is hard work, unless it is something you are deeply passionate about. When you love something, it doesn't feel like work.

If there is a job out there that you will truly love to do, nothing can stop you from getting it. You'll stalk the CEO, send free reports, create endless lists of ways they can improve their business, be a fan on their page and reply to all their customer complaints on their behalf for free. You will stop at nothing to get that job that you want.

By getting yourself into the 'sell yourself' mindset, you have a greater chance of getting that better job that reflects your passion.

Even so, perhaps you're not ready to move, or you're okay to start with a lower level position that doesn't reflect your passion, just to get that first job.

You're not alone. Of course, many of us can't find the job we want and settle for the job we need to pay the bills. And so, work tends to be hard, tiring, exhausting, depressing, and soul destroying. Even so, keep positive about the fact that the job is paying the bills.

Having said that, if you're not prepared to work hard at a job you don't like, you're going to find it particularly hard to sit at home for 10 hours a day preparing cover letters, resumes and getting ready for interviews. But it must be done, just as that job you really don't want to do would need to be done.

And so, here is what you need to know and prepare, to be able to apply for that first job. Resumes, cover letters, and interview answers.

Advertising Tool A: Resumes / CVs

A resume is a piece of paper (or pdf) that gives someone an idea of what you can offer a business. It is not just a simple list of skills. It is a complicated selling tool.

Just like any ad you see online does its best to encourage you to click on it, so too your resume needs to encourage someone to email or call you. You need to write your resume to really sell yourself. It's your selling tool for getting them to think about buying the product – you!

If you've never prepared a resume before, or are unsure of the specifics of what goes into it, here is a quick overview. There is no standard resume as every business is looking for someone different. So, don't worry if your formatting is a bit off, or you miss a paragraph. However, there is some specific information your resume must have to be able to encourage an employer to read it.

Resume contents
In countries, such as the USA, Australia, the UK, Ireland, Canada and New Zealand, a resume must have the following:

1. Personality profile – a description of what you are like and what you know in just a few lines

2. A list of jobs you've had before, along with details of your responsibilities.

3. A list of skills you've acquired through various training courses

4. A sentence at the bottom that says: 'Referees available on request'

5. If you're new to the workforce you should also include an 'Objectives' paragraph at the top, mentioning the business you are sending your application to. Including the company name is standard practice in Japan and, when utilized in the USA by Japanese, has attracted positive responses and job interviews (according to a number of my Japanese friends.)

In most Asian countries, businesses will also want you to include a photograph of yourself, a copy of your degree, birth certificate, marital status, how many children you have, and your religion. Some countries require you to include your birth ID number. I'm not familiar with Europe, Scandinavia, South America or Africa, but I doubt there would be much more than that.

A note regarding criminal records
It would depend on your crime and the jurisdiction you're in. If you think it is relevant and want to be honest, you'll need to list your criminal record. Of course, if your criminal record is stealing, rape, murder, violence or other crimes that might impact the business, you probably won't be able to get the job.

But if it is a charge for drink driving, manslaughter, taking drugs, hacking, or soft forms of crimes, then you shouldn't be discriminated against.

Some countries also allow for criminal records to be left off resumes if they have no relevance to the job. I would have no problem hiring someone who had done their time, hadn't been re-convicted of anything in a while, and the crime was something accidental, if they had the skills I needed.

I would be wary of hiring someone who was violent or angry and had committed violent, angry crimes, unless they could prove they had successfully passed an anger management course and got in touch with their softer side. Of course, I'm not a lawyer, judge or your local legal representative. I have no experience in these matters. Please investigate this important issue yourself.

Having said that, many people who have done their time, even for horrible crimes, have been able to move forward and get jobs again. Generally, the government can help in this regard and has services for helping people reintegrate into society. A criminal record, jail time, and other things that you might have done in the past, that you have atoned for in the past, should not stop you from getting a general job in the future, it may just prevent you from getting specific jobs. And, if you know it will, due to your individual circumstances, then your best bet is to start your own business and do freelance consulting work or selling your services online, where you shouldn't usually have a company have to go through detailed police checks to use your services.

Optional Resume Sections

Optional sections you may wish to add, if you think it might sell you into the job you want, is an objectives paragraph (under your personality profile) and a list of your hobbies, interests, and clubs you are a member of.

If you've been working for a while, you may have amassed quite a long list of jobs. The employer isn't really interested in anything earlier than five years ago, unless it is highly relevant to the job.

Unless you're applying for a senior management role, or a CEO position, a long resume is just going to hold you back. Keep it to two pages, and reduce the list of responsibilities in the less relevant jobs, and increase the list of responsibilities in the jobs that are more relevant.

Ten years would probably be the maximum, but know that most employers haven't got the time to read through an entire resume, and will only look closely at yours if the first couple of paragraphs catches their eye.

In recent years, only a one-page resume has been necessary. See if you can reduce it to one page. If it isn't possible, keep it to no more than two.

In more digitally savvy areas, a resume isn't needed at all. Just text your social media pages links via their app, and the employer might judge you purely on your digital presence.

On the following pages are examples of resumes. (Names and details changed to protect the privacy of the resume owners.) These resumes helped these people to get the interviews which led to the jobs they wanted.

Look over these resumes and note any extra details or features that you may not yet have added to yours.

Examples to help you

A Teacher's Resume,
A Software Engineer's Resume,
A Bad Social Media Marketer's Resume,
A Good Social Media Marketer's Resume

--

Resume of Susan Foreman
76 Totters Lane, London, UK, W1A 1AA Phone: +44 580 44 684 884 Email: susanforeman2150@g*ail.com

Professional Profile summary

Several years as an administrator and personal assistant, as well as over five years running my own childhood teaching and childcare business. Well-organized self-starter with strong interpersonal and customer service skills. Able to adapt easily to various situations and can work either as part of a team or independently as required. A passion for teaching and training, I have worked at Gene Eric English School as a personal tutor and group teacher for more than 6 months.
Employment History

2016 - Present   Gene Eric English School
Portland Place, London, W1A 1AA, UK
Position: Private and Group English Teacher
•   Developing exercises and preparation of lessons
•   Teaching students in a classroom situation at the premises of Gene Eric English School
•   Teaching students privately in various offices around Sydney, targeting individual needs
•   Assisting various students with improving their grammar, pronunciation and social conversation skills.
•   Acting as adviser to Dr John Smith.
•   Being facilitator of various extracurricular activities such as study tours and

discussion groups

2014 - 2016   **Sidrat International Pty Ltd**
                     5 Trafalgar Square, London, WC2N 5NJ, UK
                     Position: Workshop Facilitator and administrator
•   Conducting workshops with customers and non-customers across various
industries
•   Giving presentations and compiling reports on participant's contributions and
performance
•   Assisting in organizing rosters, schedules;
•   Various administrative duties

2010 – 2014   **Fawlty Towers Pty Ltd**
                     16 Elwood Avenue, Torquay, TQ1 1DR, UK
                     Position: Underwriting Administrator
•   Communicating with clients across a broad spectrum of the multicultural
community
•   Liaising with Principle and Senior Underwriters
•   Organizing functions, meetings and presentations
•   Various administrative duties including typing letters of offer and propagating
spreadsheets

2006 – 2010   **Early Childhood Teaching Service**
                     Manager and Teacher
•   Created and supplied English language lessons and cross-curriculum activities
and exercises to children aged 0-5
•   Liaised with parents and teachers regarding children's' development
•   Promotion and marketing
•   Various administrative duties

Education
Institution   Level
UK Training Academy TESOL Certificate Adv. Diploma
UK University   Bachelor of Arts Degree – (Major: Eng Lit.)
UK University   Early Childhood Studies Diploma (100 hours school teaching)

Other skills
Proficient in Windows 10, and Microsoft Office 2016, Adobe products, and various
cloud services. Familiar with Facebook, Twitter, Instagram, Snapchat and others.
Touch Typing: 60wpm. Languages spoken: English, Italian (Intermediate), Japanese
(Beginner)
Interests and hobbies

Travelling, swimming, music, socializing and meeting new people, reading,
computers, internet. Member of various teaching associations.

References

References Available on Request

--

A Software Engineer's Resume

Curriculum Vitae
From the month ended January 2018

Contact Details

Name:	**Tom Lee**
Address:	**7 Baker St Silverwater NSW 2128 Australia**
Phone:	**02 9294 4453**
Mobile:	**0414-727-427**
Email Address:	**tomlee1993@i*ug.com.au**

Career Objectives

I am seeking a career that is both challenging and fun within the I.T. industry. I thoroughly enjoy talking to customers and providing friendly and reliable service. I am an extremely easy-going person, a strong team player as well a great leader with a good eye for detail. I have a strong background in computing and I am fluent in Cantonese.

Education/Qualifications

Institution:	Macquarie University
City/Country:	Sydney/Australia
Qualifications:	Master of Commerce in Information and Systems Technology
Completed:	2016

Institution:	Macquarie University
City/Country:	Sydney/Australia
Qualifications:	Bachelor of Technology (Information & Communication Sciences)
Completed:	2013

Employment History

Macquarie University - CFL

Start Date:	October 2013
End Date:	Current
Position/Title:	Computer Services Officer
Responsibilities:	

- Provide first and second level help desk support to department of 40 staff.
- Advanced troubleshooting for PC and Mac environment
- Regularly set up databases for departments using MYSQL.

- Network and Server administration within the department
- Liaise with suppliers when new hardware or software is required
- Maintain backup of files and images of computers

Travel Indochina
Start Date: January 2013
End Date: October 2013
Position/Title: Product Coordinator
Responsibilities:
- Regular correspondence to International partners for latest airfare tariffs, hotel rates and tour rates.
- Intermediate Internal IT support, resolving any computer issues staff may have.
- Database management and maintenance
- Reservation Systems software development.
- Product website development and maintenance

Skill Summary

Strong communication skills, analytical and creative, excellent organizational and time management skills, takes responsibility and meets deadlines, a vital team player with a strong customer focus.

Computer Skills: MS Word; Advanced   MS PowerPoint; Advanced   MS Excel; Advanced
Windows (All versions); Advanced
Mac (All versions); Advanced
Linux (Several versions); Intermediate

Programming Skills: C Programming; Advanced, Python; Advanced, PHP; Advanced, HTML; Advanced, Java; Intermediate; Visual Basic; Intermediate

Languages

Fluent Cantonese
Basic Mandarin – La Lingua Language School certified

Interests

I enjoy playing tennis, mahjong, reading, socializing and relaxing.

Referees

Excellent references are available upon request.

--

So, very different people with very different lifestyles, interests, skills, ambitions and experience, but with resumes that contain much the same thing. Take some ideas from both, and put your own resume together.

To give you a better idea of the difference between a good resume and a bad one, I've created two here for you.

--

Bad Resume sent for a social media promotion job

Work Notes
Name: Eddie Munster
Address: 1313 Mockingbird Lane, Mockingbird Heights, California, 90210
Contact: +1 818-655-5000

Objectives
To get muny to life. I need money pay bills and job will help me. I want improve my skills so job can give me.

Personality
I'm friendly, outgoing person. I love frogs. I also like playing mud and gambling and drinking and using Facebook.

Work Experience
Deliver the Mockingbird Local to houses. Made friends with neighbors.
Deliver flyers, leaflets, pamphlets using bike. Some mine.
Sell lemonade. Own recipe. Made some ads.
Made a group through Minecraft
Made a Facebook group about Minecraft and playing Minecraft then putting it on YouTube.

Study
Degree in social media

--

This resume would be thrown away, deleted, or not even received.

Here is a rewrite to better attract an employer. See how much you can really say about something. If you find that it is difficult to expand on what you know, or to sell yourself, please find someone that can help you asap!

--

Good resume sent for a social media job

Curriculum Vitae
Edward Munster
1313 Mockingbird Lane, Mockingbird Heights, California, 90210
+1 818-655-5000 | Facebook: EMinester13 | Instagram: Minester13 |
eminester13@gmail.com

Objectives

Using my unique social media experience and networking abilities to help Social Medias R Us Pty Ltd to increase its market share in the world. The company fascinates me and I would love to bring my passion for what I enjoy into a business that has the potential to be a market leader.

Personality

I'm a friendly outgoing person with many hobbies and interests. I love social media and I count myself as an influencer, with a network of thousands of fans. I love people and love helping people interested in social media marketing.

Work Experience

2016-2018   Minester Group on Facebook and YouTube
                Position: Owner / Manager
o   Maintaining a Facebook fan group of over 200,000 Minecraft users
o   Researching problems and responding to solutions. Applying Mods.
o   Maintaining a YouTube channel featuring videos of Minecraft action
o   Recording, editing and voicing the videos that are uploaded to YouTube
o   Generating over a million views of my Minecraft videos
o   Generating $100,000 in advertising revenue in 1 year

2015-2016   Mockingbird Advertising Services Pty Ltd (MAS)
                Position: Letter Box delivery
                1000 Mockingbird Lane, Mockingbird Heights
o   Receiving weekly deliveries of leaflets, pamphlets, flyers and more
o   Sorting into the correct delivery times and days
o   Rebundling for easy delivery from my vehicle
o   Monitoring addresses which show 'no junk mail' or other similar signs
o   Writing feedback for MAS regarding box owners changing preferences
o   Creating my own printed ads and including them with deliveries

2014-2015   Mockingbird Local Newspaper
                Position: Paperboy
                1 Mockingbird Lane, Mockingbird Heights
o   Receiving daily deliveries of stock
o   Monitoring stock levels
o   Returning unsold newspapers
o   Updating customer lists
o   Confirming inserts and special products went to the appropriate customer

- o Customer enquiries and upselling
- o Monitoring changes in customer orders
- o Delivering newspapers

2013-2014   Lemonades R Us
Position: Manager
1313 Mockingbird Lane, Mockingbird Heights
- o Producing and supplying cups of lemonade to residents at an established location
- o Promoting and marketing lemonade through social media such as Facebook
- o Using the Facebook Boost system to advertise to a wider area
- o Collecting money, maintaining accounting spreadsheets, monitoring cash flows
- o Ensuring a high standard of hygiene in preparation of the lemonade and ice
- o Created repeat business through my network of residents
- o Increased business through word of mouth recommendations

Education
Mockingbird University: Bachelor's Degree in Communications, majoring in Social Media Advertising

Other skills
Advanced use of Facebook, Instagram, YouTube, Snapchat, Skype, Line, WeChat, WhatsApp, Weibo, and other online social media and messaging services. Expert in Microsoft Office, Windows 10, Movie Maker, Adobe Photoshop and other graphic design services.

References
Available on request

--

As you can see from the update, the resume is now much more attractive to an employer, and he or she is more likely to read it and consider Edward for the position.

Some notes
• If you're older than thirty, and living in a westernized country, you don't need to list the dates for the courses you've studied. You need to remove things from your resume that give employers an idea of your age.

• If you are printing your resume and plan to post it, or hand it in personally, print your resume on special paper. At least 100gsm, perhaps in a pastel shade like light pink or light blue. It might cost a bit more but it'll stand out in the pile and be more noticeable, especially when they're flipping through a large pile of them. Parchment paper is also good, depending on the job you're applying for. Obviously, if your applying for a graphic design job, then your cloud service containing your gigabytes of projects is what they want to see.

• Make sure your grammar, punctuation, spelling, formatting, and style are correct and consistent.

• Creating a video introduction about yourself may seem like an old idea, people have been doing it since the mid-90s on VCDs and DVDs, but it is still relevant today. These days you can create a simple one on your mobile and upload it to YouTube. Include the link on your resume at the top of the page above the Objectives or Personal Profile sections. Of course, if your video is going to show your potential employer that you're probably over fifty, then you may not want to do this.

• Whatever you write on your resume must be interesting to the person who reads it. Make sure your potential employer sees the details of the responsibilities you've had in your previous jobs and it might get them excited about hiring you, as you've had the experience that they're looking for.

NB: You are not a jigsaw piece. No one perfectly fits into a job. No ad covers everything. No resume covers everything. No interview covers everything. Put that resume together to match the ad that you're looking at, including any relevant experience that answers the questions that the employer has asked in their ad, and you're already halfway to a positive response.

Now that you've updated your resume to be more exciting, comprehensive, and something that sells you, it's time to put together that cover letter.

Advertising Tool B: Cover Letters

Some businesses no longer need them. Some businesses even just call agencies with a list of 10 points and randomly hire anyone who fits without even seeing their resume. There are even apps now where the coordinators vet the workers, then the business owner just clicks the hire button, no interview needed.

But some businesses still require them.

Your cover letter should respond to everything that is listed in the ad, point by point. Why? Because agencies have automatic detection and deletion software. If you apply online for a job saying "I've had two years' experience in x industry, but the ad says that they require five years' experience in x industry, the software will simply delete your resume without it actually being seen by any human.

In Australia, jobs advertised online may attract about one hundred applications. In the USA, a job advertised online might attract a thousand. In China, a job ad might attract a million. Imagine you're the one person that must sift through between a thousand and a million resumes! It's impossible, so software deletion programs make things a bit easier.

You need to get past these software programs and so the best thing to do is to write a detailed cover letter for every ad you apply for, and rewrite your resume to specifically reflect what each business wants in their employee. If you've included an objectives paragraph in your resume, make sure you also include the full name of the business that you wish to apply for within that objective paragraph. Always check your resume copy before sending it to each business and change the business name every time in the objectives paragraph.

Now you know why you need an entire day to just send five resumes and cover letters! It's also the reason I strongly recommend you follow up with any company you've submitted to, to make sure they've got it. Not just because it may have got lost, but because it might have been auto-deleted.

One other thing about cover letters. It's important, once you've decided you'd like to apply for a job, once you have your resume organized, that you research the company you're applying to and adapt your templates to match.

If you know a lot about them beforehand, it'll change the nature of your cover letter. Research, research, research. Find out the CEOs name, last year's profit, how many employees they have, any other relevant statistics that may influence how you write your cover letter.

It will also be useful in the interview. Employers love to know that the person in the chair knows about their business. It proves they're not just there to get money. Get them thinking that you're one of those people by including some facts in the cover letter.

Let's look at a recent job ad, and write a cover letter for it.

--

Ad:
Transcriptionist Required for Busy City Office
National transcription company
CBD location
Competitive remuneration

Transcriptionists R Us is a leader in the transcription industry with a longstanding history of providing recording and transcription services throughout the world.

We are seeking a transcriptionist to join our office.

In this role, you will listen to audio and video recordings and, strictly adhering to style guides, type accurate transcripts of them.

Five day a week positions are available and training is provided.

Transcriptionists R Us is an equal opportunity employer and offers a competitive remuneration and flexible working hours.

In your application, please briefly address or demonstrate the essential selection criteria.

Essential Selection Criteria

Typing speed of 70 wpm;
Excellent hearing;
Outstanding literacy skills, including comprehension, spelling and grammar;
Able to consistently follow formatting and/or style guidelines;
Reliable and punctual;
Able to maintain accuracy while working to deadlines;
Positive and cooperative;
Willing to undergo high-level security clearance and psychometric testing.

Desirable Criteria

Experience in a similar role will be well-regarded but is not essential;

If this sounds like the opportunity you have been looking for, then please submit your application to Geronimo using the pink APPLY FOR THIS JOB button.

--

Suggested Cover Letter

Dear Geronimo

I am interested in the job advertised on the Jobs R Us website on 23/11/2017. Job ID number 10011/002

In a variety of jobs that I have enjoyed as a temp, I have been required to transcribe my manager's recordings, as well as take dictation. (I am experienced in short-hand) I very much enjoyed this aspect of the job, and it is exciting to know that there is a position available where I could do this every day.

My typing speed is 70wpm and I have excellent hearing. My English skills are advanced as I studied literacy in university, and I am easily able to follow formatting and style guides. As a side note, three of my previous receptionist jobs required the use of different style guides, and I could adapt to all of them. Deadlines are not stressful for me as I love working under pressure, and have met all the deadlines I've been set in the past.

I am a reliable and punctual person and am conscious of always arriving before the start time and being ready to start on time, if not before.

You'll also find that I am positive and cooperative, able to fit into any business culture, with a friendly and joyful outlook on life. I would be happy to take a psychometric test to further prove this.

I understand that the files I transcribe would be sensitive in nature, with confidentiality required. I am exemplary at discretion and I would certainly be prepared to undergo high-level security clearance for the sake of the business and your clients.

Attached is my resume for your consideration.

I am available for an interview at any time convenient for you. Please feel free to contact me via email – coswald1986@gmail.com or call me on 580 44 684 884.

I look forward to hearing from you

Yours sincerely

Clara Oswald

--

This cover letter may be formatted differently, depending on how you send it. But it addresses the points in the ad quite succinctly, and is more than likely to be read by the employer or agent looking for someone like Clara.

Can you see how points in the ad were easily woven into the letter body?

NB: Writers say you should reduce the amount of 'I's in your cover letter. Sometimes that's not possible and you'll be wasting your life trying to rewrite sentences to remove an I. Work on writing the entire cover letter first, and if you find you can change a few sentences around after you finish, do it. Otherwise, send that cover letter with its resume asap and move on to the next one. The person reading it isn't going to get a bad feeling about so many uses of I.

If the ad is quite short, and you really don't know what to say in your cover letter, here is a standard template you can take some ideas from. Note some of the useful expressions in this letter.

Printed letter (Drop everything above 'Dear' for emails or online forms)

Your Name
Your Address 1
Your Address 2
Your contact numbers
Your email address

Recipients name
Recipient's position
Recipient's address
_____2018

Dear _____

I wish to apply for the position of _____ that was advertised in/on _____ on the _____ 2018. Reference number: _____

Following is a summary, addressing the points in the advertisement, to help you make a fast decision.
_____
_____

My resume is also attached.

My qualifications include _____.

You will find that I am career minded and have good administration, correspondence, accounting and general office experience. I am mature minded, enthusiastic, reliable, hard-working, friendly and keen to learn.

In addition to this, I am self-motivated with strong interpersonal communication and customer service skills, and can work under pressure in a team environment, or unsupervised if required.

Skills I possess include extensive experience in Word, Excel and various Windows operating systems as well as many Internet and mobile applications. My touch-typing speed test result is approximately 60wpm.

I would be happy to attend an interview via phone or at your office to discuss my application further, at any time that is convenient to you. You can call me on my mobile _____ or send an email to _____. I'm also available on mobile applications: Line, KakaoTalk, Skype and Wechat via ID: _____

Thank you in advance for taking the time to consider my application. I look forward to hearing from you soon.

Yours faithfully

(Your signature)
(Your name)
P.S. If this position has been taken, please keep me on file for any suitable positions that may arise in the future.

--

This is the cover letter template I have used to teach thousands of students and coach hundreds of people looking for a job. The cover letter doesn't look like the template once the student has put their own information in it.

Here is how it was changed after discussion with one of my students. Alonso got the interview, then the job after using this cover letter.

--

Medical Job Cover Letter

Alonso Frame
54/40 Turlough St Riverwood
Home Phone: (02) 9555 5555

Ms Astrid Peth
Supply Department
St Clara Public Hospital
406 Victoria Street
Darlinghurst NSW 2010

23rd November 2013

Dear Ms Peth

I would like to send forward my application for the advertised Materials Coordinator position.

I have been working in the hospital for over 4.5 years and in the past year I have been working in Xavier stores as a Materials Co-Ordinator.

In this position, I have scanned imprests barcodes, and received, stored, picked and delivered stock from the inventory to scanned areas. If problems are encountered with these responsibilities, the team comes together to find solutions. I have also enjoyed working overtime performing stock takes and other duties, which I conducted autonomously.

The work is exciting as I am doing many different tasks at the same time, as well as providing quality service in making sure that the system continues to run smoothly. For example, informing ward Nursing Unit Managers of items placed on backorder and their expected arrival dates so that it helps them to decide whether they need to get the items through alternative ways.

I have good oral and written communication skills and a strong attention to detail, as well as the time management abilities to meet deadlines under pressure. I am also self-motivated with strong interpersonal and customer service skills.

I have a certificate in Work Cover First Aid which I believe is very useful for this position. I am computer literate, with experience in Word, Excel and Windows as well as many Internet programs. My typing speed is 40 words per minute.

Attached is my resume for your consideration.

I would be happy to attend an interview with you to discuss my application further. You can call me either on my home number (02) 9555 555 or on my mobile 0404 257 387 or email: alonsoframe08@yahoo.com

Looking forward to hearing from you soon and thank you for your attention.

Yours sincerely,

Alonso Frame
--
This is just one of many ways you can change the template cover letter into something more specific to your needs.

You can start!
You now have your resume and cover letter ready. You're now ready to search for jobs in the traditional way.

If you'd prefer to search for jobs the modern way, installing apps and sending a quick text note with links to your multimedia and social profiles online, go to the resources section at the end, install the appropriate apps and start texting. (It's a lot easier, but now there is a lot more competition this way. The more traditional way of resumes and cover letters still works!)

A little bit later I go into your daily plan for job hunting. But before we get there, you'll need a bit of preparation for that surprise phone interview!

Communication Tool A: Phone Interview Skills

The worst thing about phone interviews is that you can't see the other person speaking to you. You can't see their reaction. And if you're like me and have trouble hearing people on a mobile, when there are other noises about, you might miss an important question and sound like you're playing for time when you ask them to repeat it again.

I really dislike phone interviews. And so, I've researched the best way to deal with them so that they are less nerve wracking and more controllable.

Getting ready for a phone interview, top five tips

1. Set aside a time during the daytime on a weekday when you know you won't be disturbed. Make this your 'phone call interview time.' When they email to organize a phone interview, do your best to schedule the phone interview in this period. If you can't, then move things around in your own life to make it a quiet period when they call. Send out flat mates, put out the pets, turn everything off, tell everyone not to come home or call you at that time. Avoid the period 2.30pm to 3.30pm. This is when everyone's circadian rhythm tends to drop and you'll feel sleepy no matter what you do. If you can, organize that telephone interview between 9am and 12pm, when you're most alert period.

2. Have a table ready with a glass of water, a pen, some blank paper, and a copy of your cover letter and resume. If it is likely to be a long interview, make sure your chair is comfortable and you've already been to the toilet. If it is a short interview, stand up to answer the questions.

3. Be alert. Get plenty of sleep the day before. Have a coffee, or something else with caffeine in it (if you can). Make sure you haven't had anything the day before or even a few hours before that might slow down your thinking, such as alcohol, pasta or anything with gluten and dairy in it. Take some deep breaths to get oxygen to the brain. Perhaps do some pushups or sit ups to get you even more alert, depending on your health.

4. Have a list of common phone question answers ready. If they're likely to ask you about your recent successful goals, your strengths and weaknesses, your plans for the future, have those in front of you prepared.

5. Make sure your phone is fully charged and will be able to be used for at least an hour.

During the phone interview, top five tips

1. Smile the entire time you are speaking. The sound of your voice changes when your mouth is wider with a smile, and the person on the other end will recognize it. See if you can get some happy laughs in at the appropriate times too.

2. Answer all questions with lots of detail. No yes or no. Lots of information. That's what they want to hear. Talk and talk and talk until they interrupt you. No pauses. No ums and ahs. Use the 50/50 rule, unless you have someone who wants to talk. You talk 50 percent of the time, they talk fifty percent of the time. Answer your questions with detail but avoid going over two minutes of speaking, if possible.

3. Answer the questions in ways that they want to hear. Not 'I want to work in your job so that I can learn more about the field' as that suggests it's about you. Make it about them. 'I want to work in your job as I feel my experience would be of great benefit to your team and I'd really like to help your business grow.'

4. Listen carefully to all the questions. Don't jump in half way. Always think about what you heard. Don't miss anything. I have lost count of the amount of times people simply haven't listened to my questions. Here's an example: 'Do you like paintings?' The answer to this question is usually, 'Yes, I like painting and have painted many pictures.' But that isn't the answer I wanted. I wanted 'Yes, I like paintings and some of my paintings are by such artists as Leonardo Da Vinci and Vincent Van Gogh." Using a sentence like this in an initial part of chit chat before the full interview begins will usually tell the interviewer straight away that this interview is going to be a problem. Try not to make too many mistakes in the beginning!

5. Confidently answer with a strong voice. Loud, confident people are instantly perceived as being more intelligent than quiet, shy people. Boom that personality out. Laugh into the phone. Get them really excited to meet you. If you're too shy to sell yourself on the phone, how are you going to sell yourself in person?

At the end of the call, see if you can close the deal.
Ask about an in-person interview.
Ask about when you will know.
Ask about when you should call again to find out whether another interview is needed.

If they say something like 'ah, well, we've got lots of potential candidates so, we'll be in touch,' then that means it didn't go too well and you can focus on preparing your next cover letter and resume.

If they say 'well, you've been one of the strongest candidates so far so I'll put your name in with the others when I speak with the manager tomorrow and, if you make the short list, we'll arrange an in-person interview next week' it sounds hopeful, so thank them, hang up, do a little dance, then focus on preparing your next cover letter and resume!

On rare occasions, a second interview may be scheduled at the end of a phone call. It's unlikely, though. They usually need to do about ten to twenty phone interviews, then work through their notes to work out which ones are the most likely ones to call in. You're more likely to hear about the next interview by email.

So, what sort of questions are you likely to be asked in a phone interview?

There are hundreds of thousands of possible questions! No book lists them all. No human can be prepared for all of them. And in recent times phone interview questions have been crazy, like 'If you could be a cupcake, what type of cupcake would you be?' 'If you were stranded on a desert island with a rat and a pineapple, which one would you eat first?'

However, there are some standard ones that many interviewers like to ask. I've listed them on the next page.

Phone interview questions are like in-person interview questions in a lot of cases, so I've combined them.

Your best bet is to familiarize yourself with these questions, figure out appropriate answers to them with the business that you're applying to in mind, and practice answering them in a role play situation in front of a mirror or with a friend.

Communication Tool B: Answering Skills

Some Interview Questions and Suggested Answers

How did you find out about this job?
I was researching my favorite industry when I discovered your ad on
_____ website. The job looked very attractive and it is something I can

do so I thought I had better not miss the opportunity, so I applied.

Why are you leaving your current job?
To be honest, I was only using a small part of my skills in my previous job and I felt it was a bit restrictive. With your company, I'd be able to use all my skills and be able to help more people.

What are your strengths and weaknesses?
Well, for strengths I'd have to say that I'm a hard worker, I'm friendly, I never give up on anything, and I always want to give my best. For weaknesses, I'm not sure. Maybe I can be too much of a perfectionist?

Do you prefer working alone or in groups?
I'm happy working in either. There are benefits to both and I enjoy both working by myself and with other people.

What is the most important thing that you want in a job?
It's important for me to be passionate about my job. I want to be able to put my whole self into it. With this position, I believe I would be able to do that.

What did you like about your last job?
The friendliness, the family atmosphere, the comradery, were all good. I had no problem working there but, when you know it's time to move on, its time.

What education have you had that would be useful in this job?
I keep myself updated. A number of people in my field post YouTube videos, send email newsletters and publish magazines that keep me up-to-date. For more technical aspects I attend any update course necessary to keep myself on the cutting edge of change.

What are your career goals?
I have always planned to be the best in my field and I know I could do that here. I'd like to be the person your customers call, and help your business be successful. Of course, I'm thinking about myself here, too. When your company is successful and I've brought you extra profits, it'll translate into higher salaries for me and my colleagues. So, my career goal is working here and making a success of it.

Where will you be in five years' time?
I'd really like to be in a senior position here. Perhaps a supervisor or even a manager. I'm hard working so I know I'm capable of that and am happy to do any training to achieve that.

Describe yourself for me.
[Describe yourself in positive terms listing much the same as what you listed in your personal profile and cover letter.]

Would you rather write a report or tell someone directly?
I'd be happy to do both depending on the situation. For small things that require a moment of discussion I would rather talk. For more complicated situations were a lot of data is required to be able to decide, I think a written report would be more efficient.

Do you feel stressed in your present job?
No, I don't. There is pressure, of course. We have deadlines to meet. But everyone works efficiently and I know how to get the best out of people for the project, so stress doesn't get to me.

What was the most successful thing you've done in the past year?
There was a project that everyone was having trouble finding the solution to so I called on a few people in my industry and discussed the issue with them. We came back with a solution that was within budget and we could finalize the project and make a lot of money for the company as a result.

What did you do in the last year that was a failure?
I regret to say that there was a project that we missed out on purely because we didn't really understand what the customer wanted. We prepared at least ten different solutions for them and they weren't happy with the price, so we couldn't take the project. I just know we did our best but we did regret missing out on that one.

What event or person greatly influenced your self-development?
I'm influenced by many people who are changing the world. I am passionate about doing something that will make a lasting impression on people. I like to help people and I always look at the big picture, so most business people who also look at the big picture, like Bill Gates, Elon Musk, Oprah Winfrey – these people push me to achieving greatness in everything I do.

Notes

This is just a very tiny selection of questions with one of many possible answers for each one. You will get a lot more. Search online for hundred-page lists of possible interview questions and practice answering them.

If you have a specific industry that you wish to work for, you're sure to find interview questions for that industry. With hundreds of thousands of industries, it's not possible for me to include the millions of questions that can be asked, so searching Google or Bing with long tail keywords about what job you're looking for, is my best recommendation for you.

The STAR method

I also recommend you search online for answers using what is known as the STAR method. Situation, Task, Action, Result. These questions are usually asked of people applying for higher level positions - above junior level or above internship level, but it's best to be prepared. Essentially, they need answers specific to your previous job, so only you would be able to provide the best answer. It's a way for employers to get original answers from you, rather than memorized ones.

Here's an example STAR method question and answer:

If you are given an important project that is due tomorrow, but time has run out to work on it today, would you keep working or would you wait until morning?
(Situation) I had a situation like that in my previous job. We had to get a large volume of papers scanned for a legal case. The company only gave us 3 days to do it, but we had limited scanning machines and staff. *(Task)* My manager requested us to work as long as we could, so several of us did just that. We had to finish what would normally take a week in under 48 hours. *(Action)* So, we ended up working, with only minor breaks, for 36 hours straight, taking each letter-sized piece of paper and feeding it into a machine, checking it was scanned correctly then putting in another one. With the main section done, it was up to the next team to finalize it, so I then simply passed out in my manager's office! We got the project done in time. *(Response)* What I learnt from this changed my view on work, and I realized that just about anything was possible. So, I'm happy to work if there is a deadline, and I'll keep working until it is done.

True story!

Now that you have completed that section

Congratulations!

You now have all the tools to move up to the next level.

Add 2,000 points and level up!

Level 7
Change Yourself

It's now time to create your own working week. You are the master of your time so you will know the best way to start, but this may be your program for the next 21 days. If have other responsibilities, you'll need to work those into this schedule.

By setting yourself to this schedule now, you become more employable. You'll be able to easily slip into your work role when you get it.

Employers can tell when someone has been out of work for a while - sloppy dressing, unkempt hair, tired eyes - and it makes it harder for the employer to consider them for the job, especially when the next interviewee has focused attention, awake eyes, and a healthy, active look. So, you need to cultivate this look.

Following this schedule will quickly put you in the working mindset and the employer will be more likely to consider you. By the end of just the first week, you'll be a completely different person, and you'll already be thinking about how you can be even more evolved by the second week!

As you learn a new thing, implement a new thing, follow a new thing, you'll see more new things come into your reality that you will feel you wish to add to yourself, to your personality, to your behavior. It's an absorption process. Following this schedule will enable you to upgrade yourself.

Your new job search schedule

Monday
6am - Up, breakfast, shower, other morning things, get into your best office clothes, and sit down at your own computer as though you're at work. If you need to have coffee and snacks ready next to you, get that ready. Be ready as though you'll suddenly have an interview with only five minutes to prepare. (If you're a night shower person, change to morning showers asap. Potential employers want you smelling fresh. Get into that habit early.)

8am to 9am - Check your emails, texts and phone messages. Respond as soon as possible. Organize interviews where possible. If you are expecting a call, be prepared for it, assuming you have already been sending out cover letters and resumes before you started reading this book. Always check your emails asap. If you are an early riser (5am?) then you may have already organized this.

9am to 11am - Search for jobs. Choose one of these below to search for today. The next tomorrow, the next the following day…

Apps (Search and apply from your smart phone)
Jobmo.org, Switchapp.com, Jobrapp.com,

Websites (Search and apply from your PC)
Indeed.com, SimplyHired.com, LinkedIn.com, Jobcase.com

Niche job boards (thousands!)

Job pages on specific business sites (millions!)

You can go through niche job boards rather than the official and expensive boards when looking for a job. For a start, less people will be looking on niche boards, so that means less competition. You will have some niche boards in your area, even if it is just a few pages on Gumtree.com This list of niche boards is a bit outdated but it'll give you some ideas: smartrecruiters.com/blog/best-50-niche-job-boards/

NB: If you spend a day searching the lot for jobs and get to the end of the day without having sent a resume to anyone, you're already a day behind, and most of those jobs might have already been removed by the following day! Only search until you've found five job ads, then stop. If you find five in the first hour, don't continue searching. Stop there and start the next phase.

If you can't find any on your first app/search, move to the next one. If you can't find any in one hour, you're being too picky. In your second hour, you'll have to lower your expectations. Lower pay, further away, harder work, etc.

Having looked for jobs on job boards many times, I know how hypnotic it can be. "Maybe it'll be on the next page, maybe something better is there, I'll just click one more… Make sure you get five job ads as soon as possible, then stop.

11.00am to 11:15am Break

11:15am to 1:15pm Write and send a cover letter and a resume to job #1. If another of the five jobs is similar, send your cover letter and resume to another job. If they're all different, start work on writing the next cover letter and resume.

1:15pm to 1:45pm Lunch

1:45pm to 3:45pm Write and send a cover letter and a resume to the next job, and more where possible.

3:45pm to 4:00pm. Break

4:00pm to 6:00pm Write and send a cover letter and a resume to the next job, and more where possible

6:00pm to 7:00pm Dinner

7:00pm to 8:00pm If you have already sent five, you can move onto Admin. If you haven't, make sure you keep working until you have sent the fifth cover letter and resume. Make sure you complete five a day. Then it's…

Admin time!
Create a spreadsheet containing information about the cover letters and resumes you've sent. The type of job. The contact person. (Was it through an agency or directly?) Contact details like phone numbers. Imagine you get a random call at the end of the week from one of these jobs. What information will you need to know then? Note it down now so that you'll be prepared for unexpected calls.

8:00pm – break. Finalize everything, then get ready for bed. Do the dishes, tidy up, or whatever you do in the evening that doesn't involve a bright screen. Don't look at another screen until the next morning.

Bed by 10:00pm. Sleep before 11:00pm

Add 20 points for each cover letter/resume combination sent. If you score at least 100 points, add another 20 bonus points.

Tuesday
6am - Up. If you have a full-time job you'll need to get up at 6am anyway, so make sure you get your body clock set for this time. If you're a later riser, late sleeper like me, it might take a week or two to get adjusted. Don't start your adjustments on your first day of work! You'll have poor performance and lose your job quickly.

8:00am to 9:00am - Check emails etc. Did you get any replies from yesterday?

9:00am to 11:00am – Follow up the job enquiries. Call the contact number for each job. Ask if they received your resume. If they haven't, send it again. If they have, ask them if there's anything further they might need. They will usually quickly say something about lots of candidates, they'll be in touch, etc. If they're really interested they might ask for an interview straight away. Take the booking. Get prepared. This may change the following schedule. That's okay. Drop anything in these schedules to get ready for phone and in-person interviews.

If there are no replies, and you have not been able to contact anyone, please make sure you have noted all this in your admin sheet. Keep track of everything, including non-contact. After five days of not getting any contact from a job application, it's best to forget it. Consider five days the maximum response from any application you make. On a rare occasion, they may contact you weeks later. Don't dwell on it. Move forward. You can always say no.

11:00am to 11:15am Break

11:15am to 1:15pm Check emails again, follow up any replies received. Search for five new jobs.

1:15pm to 1:45pm Lunch

1:45pm to 3:45pm Write and send a cover letter and a resume to the next job, and more where possible

3:45pm to 4:00pm. Break

4:00pm to 6:00pm Write and send a cover letter and a resume to the next job, and more where possible

6:00pm to 7:00pm Dinner

7:00pm – 8:00pm Today should be a bit easier than Monday, now that you have your templates ready and you've got into a good habit. Tomorrow should be easier still. Do your admin then finish this kind of work for today. You're doing well!

Add 20 points for each cover letter/resume combination sent. If you score at least 100 points, add another 20 bonus points.

Wednesday

8:00am to 9:00am Now that you've sent out ten resumes, you should have started to receive emails and interview requests. Follow these up and arrange your interviews for the day.

9:00am to 11:00am Go through your list of jobs applied for and check which ones you haven't had a response from yet. Follow them up. Call, email etc. See what sort of response you can get. Schedule an interview where possible.

Just because you have interviews set, doesn't mean you'll get the job. You can't stop applying. If you haven't got any interviews scheduled, you'll need to increase the number of resumes and cover letters you send. So today, find six. If after today you still get no response, find seven on Thursday. Find eight on Friday etc. So, this period could either be searching for more jobs or attending interviews.

And just think how more confident you'll be in one interview if you know you have others lined up!

11:00am to 11:15am Break

11:15am to 1:15pm Check emails again, follow up any replies received. Search for new jobs.

1:15pm to 1:45pm Lunch

1:45pm to 3:45pm Write and send a cover letter and a resume to the next job, and more where possible

3:45pm to 4:00pm Break

4:00pm to 6:00pm Write and send a cover letter and a resume to the next job, and more where possible

6:00pm to 7:00pm Dinner

Alright, things are much easier now so, you can start to relax a bit. Get your admin up to date and start thinking about organizing other things – what you'll wear to the interview, how you'll answer the interview questions etc.

Doing some role playing is good too. If you know you're going to be interviewed for a particular job, play it through at home. Use a table and play both the manager and potential employee. Swap roles or get someone to play the part of the manager. \

This is known as hump day in many offices, so you're past half way.

Add 20 points for each cover letter/resume combination sent. If you score at least 100 points, add another 20 bonus points.

Thursday

If you haven't got an interview organized by today, you might be feeling a bit down. Don't be down. Be positive. You are learning a lot of new skills simply by implementing this plan, changing your mindset, your personal schedule. Look back over what you've achieved this week so far. You're a completely different person to last week. A time to celebrate, but not yet. Save that for Friday night!

So, today, your schedule will be the same as Wednesday. Refer to that.

Add 20 points for each cover letter/resume combination sent. If you score at least 100 points, add another 20 bonus points.

Friday

Analysis day! Now we get to finalize the week. Just like in the office where projects are finalized, put on the backburner due to the weekend, or delegated to someone else, it's time to go through your file.

By today, you should have sent out, at the very least, 20 cover letters and resumes. If you haven't received any contact at all from those 20 cover letters and resumes, then there is something wrong that needs to be looked at.

Today, you'll need to look online for resume-help gurus. Someone who can rewrite your resume. Or you'll need to review the sort of jobs you're applying for.

By this stage, everyone I have ever helped has had some kind of response from at least one of their applications, whether it is a 'no' answer or a 'we'll keep you posted' answer, or even an interview booking. Everyone. If you haven't, you'll need to look into everything you've done so far and reconsider what you're doing.

So, here's the plan for if you haven't had any responses yet:

As usual, up at 6am. Check emails, texts, calls etc.

If still no response from jobs applied for since Monday, go back to your first job ad and check the wording.

Did your cover letter answer all the questions in the job ad?
Does your resume suit the job ad?
Note any differences you find. Is the ad still online?

Try rewriting your cover letter and resume to be better, to match the ad better than before. Then reapply, if you really want the job.

What could you add or change?

You might be surprised to find that what you originally sent on Monday is now not something you would send today, purely because four days of training yourself to send resumes, and reading what employers want, has already evolved you. You're not the person you were on Monday, and so you may want to do things differently now that it is Friday.

Go through all the job ads, and pretend that you are the agent receiving the cover letter and resume. Put yourself in their shoes. If you had to find a person for that job, how would you judge your application? If you can see where the agent might have rejected it, you'll see how this can be a valuable learning experience, and how you can improve things for the next job applications.

Friday is the time to clear house. You can still call the agents or receptionists and discuss things with them. Give one final call to the jobs you applied for on Monday, and if they still haven't found someone, it might be a very long time before you get that job anyway. Highlight it as one to ignore, and move onto the next one. Clean up your Monday and Tuesday jobs on Friday. Clean up your Wednesday and Thursday jobs on Monday.

If you have been working hard throughout the week and you have sent over 20 cover letters and resumes, you don't need to send any on Friday. Friday is also the day many businesses don't bother following up their own ads, resumes received etc. So, it's unlikely you'll get a call or email regarding a job on Friday anyway. Also, it is unlikely you'll get interviews on Fridays too. The best days for interviews are Tuesdays, Wednesdays and Thursdays. (Having said that, every business is different and it would depend on who is available.)

If, however, you didn't really want any of the jobs you've already applied for, then you can simply move on to finding more jobs!

So, if you have received responses, and you have organized interviews, and things moving along smoothly, then today is simply like any other day. Send five cover letters and resumes.

Saturday and Sunday are times to do your shopping, prepare your home, get all your purchases, banking, bills etc. in order, so that you can spend the next Monday to Friday focused on getting a job. Remember, those who work full time rarely get to go to the bank, do shopping, meet their friends or otherwise complete things that those, without a job weekdays, can do.

Schedule your weekly plan so that all the things everyone else does on weekends is also what you will do on weekends. Getting into the habit of an office worker will also enable you to fit into the culture once you get there!

By the following Monday, you will have already created your own plan of what works for you, allowing for you to think about being in an office environment. You may have had new ideas come to you, new ways and better ways of doing something than what I have described here. That's great!

Keep doing that for the next three weeks, or until you get that job.

If you're in a city area, and sending out at least 20 resumes and cover letters a week that specifically fit the job, and you've followed everything in this book, then the probability is high that you should have already got a job offer. If you haven't yet, please go over the book again and see if there is anything you can improve, anything you have missed, or if you have anything that is holding you back from applying for a job.

If you have already had a phone/Skype interview, add 50 points per interview. If you have already had an in-person interview, add 100 points per interview.

Personal stories from Jason

I have used these methods to secure a job and I have been successful in getting the job that I needed when I needed it. In 1990, I went to three interviews. Accounting, Adult Services, and a Bookshop. I failed the accounting test, the Adult Services center thought I was too green, but the bookshop welcomed me with open arms.

In 1996, I went to just one interview. A stationery store. I got the job straight away. From then I began helping others get jobs by giving them advice on my experience and doing more research on interview coaching.

In 1999, I went to an IT start-up, a data entry service and a scanning company. I didn't like the IT start-up when I heard about what they were planning to do, and how disorganized it was, so I was a bit confrontational in the interview to ensure I wasn't offered it. The data entry service was from an agency but my typing speed wasn't fast enough at the time. The scanning company were impressed with my skills and I was hired and made supervisor within a year.

While taking a working holiday in the UK I applied for just one job, cheque processing at a bank, via an agent. I got it.

In 2000, I was called back to my IT job, and I took on a second job (data entry, night shift) Barely anyone wanted the position so it was easy. Even so, I really wanted to run my own business so I left that job (after they made me supervisor!) and ran a computer repair company. In that sense, every customer I saw was interviewing me for the position of fixing their computer. It was an interview a day for two years. Of course, I moved on.

In 2002, I left the IT company, continued fixing computers while starting up my ESL teaching service. In this sense, I had not only students interviewing me, but parents interviewing me for the position of teaching their kids. I only wanted to teach adults, though, so I moved over to teaching adults full time.

Every time an adult student came to me, it was an interview. They needed to know whether I would be a good teacher for them. Of course, I made things fun and interesting, and I continued to make subsequent lessons fun and interesting.

I opened a small ESL college in 2007 and closed it in 2012. In that time, I interviewed many teachers for positions there. I learnt a lot from the other side of the table. When I closed the business, I continued teaching part time, but also focused more on my interview coaching. This time students were interviewing me so that I could interview them.

Through hearing thousands of students' stories about how they couldn't get a job, I could see what they were doing wrong and how to correct it. Those that followed my advice usually got a job within a week. Those that took some of my advice were still able to get a job within a month. There were a few that didn't take my advice at all, couldn't believe I could even suggest what I suggested, and decided that getting unemployment benefits was preferable to 'selling themselves out to the corporate elite'. So, I wasn't able to help them, unfortunately.

In 2013, I decided to take a break from teaching and go back into the workforce. I decided it was a good chance to test whether my advice on getting a job still worked. I enjoyed drinking wine and decided that I would do a job that I had never done before. Sell wine via an inbound call center. I had no experience, I had no skills, I don't even like using a phone, yet, guess what, I got the job straight away. My coaching still worked!

I left in 2015 to pursue my freelance writing goals.

This overview shows you that, even though I had no degree, even though I had limited skills, I could still get a job completely unrelated to jobs I had done before. You can do that too. Keep an open mind, and jobs will become available. And remember, even if you get a job now that you don't like, it doesn't stop you looking for one that you do!

Review

1. Positive and hard-working mindset. All mental issues - solved
2. Research on the businesses you plan to apply for - completed
3. Resumes and covers letters individually targeting each business you plan to apply for - created
4. Series of questions and answers absorbed and rewritten in your way of speaking - memorized
5. A minimum of five resumes and cover letters every day - sent

Optional Extra Tools
Physical Tool: Appearance Skill

Okay. You've got a face to face interview coming up in the next few days. Now it's time to really do some renovations on yourself.

Men

• Hair washed and cut
• Nails clean
• Nose hairs trimmed
• Ear hairs trimmed
• Beard shaven or neatly shaped. (Clean-shaven is preferred for an office job.)
• Spots and cuts concealed with invisible makeup where possible.
• Clean face, non-greasy. Of course, you could always just turn up as yourself and not have to go through the whole metrosexual styling, but the impression you give is important. If you don't look like you care about yourself, how will you be able to care about the business?
• Clothing standard style for guys – suit and tie. Borrow, rent or buy. Always have a suit. Always have black shoes. (Don't ever wear any other color shoes besides black. If you think brown might be okay, look online for the research conducted in the UK about candidates wearing brown shoes being rejected by banks!)
• Shine your shoes. Give them a new coat of black polish. Be careful what you walk in on the way to the interview.
• Wear cologne or aftershave, but not too much. Just enough to disguise your normal skin scent, not enough to set off the interviewer's asthma.

Women

• Hair washed and styled, even if you plan to wear a head scarf
• Nails clean. If you like to paint your nails, choose something pastel or plain. Not too bright.
• Makeup done by a professional. Lightly, not over the top. No bright red ruby lips or green eyeshadow. Think colors that closely resemble your complexion and accentuate your unique beauty. Of course, you don't have to wear makeup, but if you don't, the impression you give is that you don't care about yourself. And if you don't care about yourself, how will you be able to care about the business?
• Clothing – suit or dark colored dress suitable for your shape. No need for low cut tops. At the end of the day the employer has to think of the bottom line so ignore the 'if you've got it, flaunt it' slogan, and don't. Also, your interviewer is most likely to be female and is unlikely to be impressed.
• Heels. No need for stilettos unless you're comfortable in them, but slightly higher heels will also give you a confidence boost. Not to mention statistics showing that the taller you're perceived to be, the higher the chance of being employed.
• Wear perfume, but not too much. Just enough to disguise your normal skin scent, not enough to set off the interviewer's asthma.

Both
• Choose clothes that conceal your tattoos.
• Remove all face and arm jewelry. (Remove wedding rings if possible. If you're a young female, you don't want the interviewer thinking you're going to have children soon.) Do not wear anything that makes a jangling noise!
• Minor weight issues – Employers don't usually notice, unless the building doesn't have an elevator
• Shower on the day of the interview, not the night before. Depending on the distance between your home and the interview, a few hours beforehand.
• Wear deodorant that has 48-hour protection. This means a higher amount of aluminum content, needed if you're nervous and likely to sweat more.
• If you need to have a cigarette before the interview, do it an hour before, then brush your teeth, and gargle with mouthwash. Or wait, and have one after the interview. Same goes for food.
• Have a mint before you go into the interview anyway. Nervousness will dry out your mouth and increase your chance of having bad breath.
• If you smoke at home, your clothes are going to smell. Avoid smoking in the house, and keep the clothes you usually wear for interviews somewhere away from cigarette smell.
• If you keep your clothes in cupboards with naphthalene (moth balls) they're going to stink of it in the interview. Either wash them a couple of days before and store them elsewhere, or air them somewhere for a few days. *(This is a pet peeve of mine and I can't stand the smell. If someone smells of naphthalene, I get someone*

else to do the interview. However, if they're likely to get the job smelling of naphthalene, it's
unlikely I'll ever have time to speak with them in person!)

• Go to the toilet before the interview, and do your best to disguise any personal smells

• Eat food that is unlikely to give you flatulence. Avoid food such as pasta, wheat, dairy, cabbage, baked beans and other things containing fiber. More on this later.

• Eat food that is unlikely to make you sleepy or less aware.

• Have a coffee or some other drink an hour before to help you stay focused and be able to quickly answer questions without thinking too much. Make sure you factor in that toilet trip before the interview, if you have caffeinated drink. Some interviews can last three hours. Show them you have staying power.

• Always, always, always wear freshly washed underclothes. Just because something looks clean, doesn't mean it smells clean. Only wear your underclothes once before washing. Please. I beg you! The amount of people that have come in for an interview having done everything else on this list but put on clothes they'd worn a few times already, have had me needing to leave the room to 'take a call.' No thanks. Please wear freshly washed and dried clothes to an interview. And make sure you wash your clothes every day. Yes, even after you get the job. Otherwise your colleagues are going to start leaving notes, and bottles of deodorant on your desk, and HR are going to call you in for 'a little chat.'

If you've done most of these things, or have already been doing all these things, add 1000 points.

Let's go into some more detail about this last point.

Body Odor and Communication

So, how does body odor affect communication? If you had to have a long discussion with someone about something, but you just can't get close enough to speak to them, you're more likely to send them an email or talk to them on the phone, which means you'll miss out on some very important body language signals that may be needed to help you make your decision. If we could do everything by email or on the phone, we wouldn't need meetings!

If you go to an interview not realizing you smell bad, no one is going to tell you, you simply just won't get the job, unless you're the only one that can do it. Yes, there are 'smelly' people that are perfect for the job. And if everyone had their own office, a smelly person wouldn't be an issue. However, we now have open plan offices with the smelly person being just one meter away from everyone else. This can cause a loss of productivity, a high turnover of staff, increased costs in retraining, and delicate human resources meetings with the offender.

In Australia, people even complain anonymously to radio stations about smelly people in their offices, and the radio station jocks would call the smelly person directly on their extension, live on air, that they're 'on the nose' and that they have to do something about it. If you've been ignoring attempts to get you to clean up your act, now's the time to change your habits in time for that all-important interview.

Ironically, Steve Jobs (one of the creators of the Apple company) was said to have been a very smelly person in his younger years, but a computer company gave him a job anyway. Most managers would not have.

Reducing Body Odor
So, what can you do in the short term to reduce body odor?
1. Change your diet
2. Shower in the morning, not night (or shower both morning and night)
3. Wash your clothes daily. Even if you decide to only wear them once, but leave them in the washing hamper for weeks before they're washed, the stains and smell won't come out easily.
4. Wash with hot water to help dissolve skin oils, caked sweat and kill bacteria and germs. Use heavy duty washing liquid. Cold water does not do as much for smells. For stubborn stains, hand wash your clothes using abrasive soap.
5. Drink plenty of water. Sometimes your skin's reaction to food hangs around in your body for days without proper hydration.
6. Exercise. Even if it is just a brisk one hour walk every day. This will get your lymphatic system working on those toxins that have built up in your body, and break them down. Shower afterwards, of course.
7. On hot days, shower regularly. If you need to take three showers in the day to stop from knocking people out with your smell, do it. Some workplaces have showers for their staff for this reason. Bring freshly washed changes of clothes to keep smelling great. (A new set of clothes every shower.) Use good smelling soap, too. Something not too abrasive if you're having more than two showers a day.
8. Make sure you wash your hair every day. The more hair you have, the greater the smell it can hold. Choose some mild shampoo and wash it every time you have a shower. (You don't need to follow the directions that say rinse and repeat. That's just a marketing tool to sell more shampoo!)

Of course, some of this advice may not work for you if you're in an area with water restrictions, and can't have more than one shower a week. But if that is true, then everyone around you will be in the same situation, so it won't make much difference. However, still schedule your restricted shower to be before that important interview.

Types of Food to Avoid
Food that causes offensive body odor when eaten excessively
1. Red meat
2. Refined white flour
3. Hydrogenated oil
4. Eggs
5. Liver
6. Fish
7. Legumes
8. Onions
9. Garlic
10. Asparagus
11. Curry
12. Coffee
13. Alcohol
14. Rancid fat
15. Tobacco
16. Any hot spices
17. Sugar
18. Dairy products, depending on body type
Eat very moderately, and drink glasses of water with every meal.

Types of Food that Reduce Offensive Body Odor
Things to have to help reduce offensive body odor
1. Parsley
2. Celery
3. Mint
4. Sage
5. Rosemary
6. Thyme
7. Oregano
8. Vitamin B
9. Zinc
10. Plenty of water!!!

Another problem that can cause bad body odor is organ failure. If you've got great olfactory senses it is possible to tell, very quickly, that someone is ill. A failing liver, for example, can cause someone to have very bad smelling skin and breath. It can be so strong as to have people gasping or choking. If this is something you've encountered, you may be saving their life if you send them to a doctor.

If you've already changed your diet, or have changed most of these things, add 1000 points.

Other Factors that May Influence a Potential Employer

Please note that your area may have different rules for interviews, or require a longer list of things you need to do to prepare for them. Here are a few examples.

South Korea
I've heard that in some businesses in the hospitality industry in South Korea, a potential female employee should have had plastic surgery when she was younger to correct any faults that the business feels may offend customers. Males should wear makeup to make themselves more attractive to customers. Photographs are mandatory, and if they don't like your photo they won't read the resume. Much like actors and actresses going for jobs in western countries.

Japan
I've heard that, in Japan, an employee must be able to commit to thirty years with the same company, and follow the lead of those who run it without question. They should also always be available seven days if the company needs them, and work at least 12 hours a day, leaving after the boss leaves. An interview is usually with multiple people, is quite long, and detailed answers are needed. In some companies, if you're female and want to have children, you must be put on a maternity schedule and wait for others in your company to have their children first before you are allowed to have yours. If you are already pregnant you won't get the job. If you get pregnant out of turn you may either lose your job, or be so offended and insulted by microaggressions against you from all the other co-workers for jumping the queue, that you'll end up leaving your job anyway. *(Now you know one of the reasons why Japan has such a low birth rate!)*

Australia
If you're male and you attend an interview in Australia, the first few chitchat questions will be about the weather, sport and drinking. If you can't answer these in a way that suggests you're used to speaking about these often, then you've failed before the interview has even begun! (You won't fit the culture

of that business, which probably has a sport watching, drinking night at the end of every week, or participates in regular sport and drinking 'bonding' sessions for colleagues.)

China

Chinese employers check worldwide university rankings, and if the university you did your HD degrees and two master's degrees don't rank high enough, then you're unlikely to be considered for an interview. If you are planning to work in China and haven't done a degree yet, aim to get a course in one of the top 50 worldwide universities, and keep track of their performance. Change universities if their ranking drops so that you have a better chance of competing against the other million or so people applying for the same job!

UK

I've read that, if you go for a job in a bank in London, and wear brown shoes or a loud tie, you won't get the job. Take the time to look up the right color tie and type and color of shoes, even how the tie should be tied, to increase your chances of getting a job.

There are a lot more unspoken things like this that may take a bit of research to find, but if you're aware of them and can plan for them, it'll give you the edge on the competition.

If you've made the effort to research what is needed in your area of the world, and have made the necessary adjustments, add 1000 points.

What else can you do to influence the employer in the interview to consider you for the position?

Change Your Body Language

Body language describes the actions your body projects that allows people to read you, without you necessarily having to speak. If you cross your arms, look to the side before speaking, scratch etc., this is all body language.

Some statistics
Body language is over 50% of communication
Pauses, sighs, intonation are over 35% of communication
Spoken language is less than 10%!!!

So, if language is such a small part of communication, you're going to need good body language skills in the office. A good manager must be able to use body language to great effect. Controlling your body language is the key to a successful career, and a person who projects confidence is more likely to move up in the world.

Imagine you're an interviewer, and you encounter the following two people waiting in the waiting room for an interview. Without speaking with them, who are you more likely to employ?

Person 1: Keeps looking at his watch. Going through his files in his briefcase. Reading over his notes. Scratching his arms. Rubbing sweat off his forehead then wiping his hands on his trousers. Fidgeting in his seat.

Person 2: Sits relaxed in the chair reading one of the office magazines

Of course, person 2.

Imagine you're at a pub. Which of these two people are you likely to say 'hi' to?

Person 1: Keeps staring at you from a distance. Looks away embarrassed, frowns, then, out of the corner of your eye you see the person looking at you again. They try to get up from their seat then they sit down again, take a gulp of their drink and get up again. They then move purposely across the room to you.

Person 2: Walks to the bar near you. Orders a drink. Stands relaxed, leaning on the bar, smiling casually, looking about the room with interest. Turns back to the person at the bar, makes small talk, laughs. Grabs their drink then comes over to you.

Of course, person 2.

As you can see from these examples, we don't need to speak with someone to be able to instantly judge them.

So, how do you change your body language?

It takes a bit of practice and there are many things you need to do, but you probably know some already. See if you can work out which is the best body language to use in these examples.

Test Your Body Language Awareness

1. If you have an appointment and the receptionist sends you in do

you...
A. Enter confidently without knocking?
B. Knock politely on the door before entering?

2. When you shake their hand do you...
A. Take their hand confidently with a strong, friendly grip and pump it twice?
B. Carefully take their hand with your clammy, sweaty one, and try not to hurt them by holding it limply?

3. When you need to sit down do you...
A. Choose your own chair?
B. Wait to be told where to sit?

4. When you want to be sincere do you...
A. Lean forward and look them in the eye?
B. Lean back and act cool?

5. When you are trying to get a point across...
A. Do you put a little bit of emotion into your voice to make things sound friendly?
B. Do you keep a steady and serious speaking rate?
C. Does your voice go up and down dramatically depending on your emotions?

6. When you're thinking do you...
A. Use prevarication expressions like "I don't have all the information regarding that issue with me but based on what I remember I can probably guess that...?
B. Say lots of ums and ahs?

7. When you're maintaining eye contact do you...
A. Keep your eyes on theirs for up to 10 seconds?
B. Keep your eyes on theirs for minutes?
C. look at their eyes for less than a second?

8. When walking down the corridor do you...
A. Keep your head up, back straight, and confidently swing your arms as you purposefully head to your next destination?
B. Look shy, look to the ground, slightly stooped posture, shuffle your feet, walk slowly?

9. When the boss tries to tell you that you did something wrong and offers advice do you?

A. Lean forward with open arms smiling and accepting the information and promising to do better next time
B. Sit in the chair looking around with crossed arms

10. When you are communicating do you...
A. Relax and reveal some of your emotions through your facial expressions and body language?
B. Keep all your emotions hidden and put on your serious face?

Answers: Did you choose mostly As?!
Add 1000 points!

Body Language and Interviews

Personal Space
When you stand next to a person do you think about their personal space? How much personal space do people need? It's not standard, and introverts need more than extroverts, Caucasians need more than Asians. You need to judge it. Best to keep a bit further away than you're comfortable with then check whether the person you're speaking to takes a step forward or back.

If they step back they need more personal space, so don't take it personally! If they step forward, decide your personal space limit. If you need to communicate with this person, stay where you are so that they are comfortable, especially if you're trying to get a job, a raise or a date! If you don't adjust, it'll disrupt your conversation.

Shaking hands
Some people are uncomfortable about shaking hands. If the person you are meeting looks like they haven't washed in a week, do you want to shake their hand? In this situation, it is not polite to shake their hands then rub your hand on your pants! Sometimes if you don't shake, it'll disrupt your conversation, so you have to do it anyway. If this is likely to be a common occurrence for you, you can always carry around antibacterial wipes.

In business in the 21st century, shaking both men and women's hands is a sign of equality. Make sure you shake everyone's hands, no matter what. An exception would be if they say that they can't due to religious observances.

Body Language Role Play

Now that you're aware of some body language expressions, it's time to use them in a role play!

Getting the body language right is more important than the words you say. It's your chance to use your acting skills! You can get two chairs and simply swap between them, being the Person then the Interviewer, or you can get a friend to help you.

Interview 1

Person A: (Standing outside a door. Knocks. Looks around.) Hi. I'm_____Is it okay if I can come in?
Interviewer: (Nodding, indicates a seat then sits when Person A sits) I'm _____As you saw outside I've got at least four people to interview today so I only have time to ask you one question.
Person A: (Frowns. Looks disappointed. Upset. Blinks several times.) Um. Er. Okay.
Interviewer: (Leans back in his chair. Puts hands behind his head. Smiles.) What do you plan to do in five years' time?
Person A: (Lifts eyebrows. Looks down at his hands. Looks up again and looks to the left of the interviewer) um. (Looks at his fingers) I'd like to be the boss of a big company like yours.
Interviewer: (Nods.) Excellent. I like people with plans. Thank you. If I have a position here for you I'll call you. You can go.
Person A: (Looks disappointed.) okay

Interview 2

Person B: (Opens the door and walks into the office. Greets the interviewer by shaking his hand, strongly. Takes a seat as the interviewer sits) Hi. I'm _____ Nice to meet you.
Interviewer: (Smiling.) Nice to meet you too. I'm_____
Person B: I saw that previous interviewees were only in here for a minute so I guess your time is short. How can I help you?
Interviewer: (Smiling broadly) Excellent. I have just one question. What do you plan to do in five years' time?
Person B: (smiling in a friendly way) I have a goal to be a manager of a department in your company. I believe my skills can make a huge improvement to your bottom line and my contributions will be so good for your company that you'll have no choice but to promote me! (gives a friendly grin)
Interviewer: (laughs) Excellent. I like your style. Thank you. If the job is yours, you'll know within the week. Thank you.
Person B: (knowing the interview is at an end, gets up out of his chair and shakes the manager's hand again) Thank you. I look forward to hearing from

you!

Interview 3

Person C: (Opens the door and slowly walks in but looks a little nervous) Good morning sir. I'm_____. (Shakes Interviewer's hand, limply) It's very nice to meet you. (Stays standing)

Interviewer: (Indicates that Person A should sit) I'm_____Please take a seat.

Person C: (Carefully sits, adjusting themselves in the chair to be more comfortable) Thank you.

Interviewer: (frowns slightly at how slow this person is) As you saw outside I've got at least ten more people to interview today so I only have time to ask you one question.

Person C: (Eyes blink. Frowns. Breathes out quietly. A flash of anger appears for a moment on their face then vanishes. Then they smile and lean back in the chair, no longer caring) Of course. I understand.

Interviewer C: Good. What I want to know is, what do you plan to do in five years' time?

Person C: (Rolls eyes) Oh, well, hopefully I'll be rich and living on an island in the Bahamas! How many people have applied for this job anyway?

Interviewer C: (Not impressed with the answer. Steely gaze.) 378 applications were received and we've chosen 25 people for interviews today.

Person C: (Looks down, annoyed. Then looks up and smiles) Okay. Well, looks like you've got a lot of work to do, then.

Interviewer C: Yes. Thank you for your time. You can go now.

Person C: (Frowns) Right. Thanks (Leaves quickly)

Of these interviews, which person is more likely to get the job?

Mirroring

Mirroring is the action of matching your personality, body language and way of speaking to the speaker. If you find that the manager you are being interviewed by is a slow speaker, then you should slow your speech. If you find they speak fast, speed up. If they have slow body language, slow yours to match. If they lean forward in their chair, lean forward to match them. Smile when they smile.

Of course, don't do all this too fast or automatically. Allow a few seconds between changes and slowly shift to a similar position and behavior so that it looks natural.

If you match someone's behavior they will be more interested in you subconsciously, and it can subtly improve your chances of your resume making it into the short list.

Bad Habits

One habit that is noticeable and usually disappears by the mid-twenties is the propensity for some people to play with their hair, chew their nails, rub their face repeatedly, and other habits that are repetitive and involve their fingers. An interview can cause an increase in these reactions and is a way for the employer to see whether you may have some bad habits that could offend or disgust both customers to the company or colleagues that sit near you.

Picking your nose, putting your fingers in your ears to remove wax, snorting, spitting, coughing phlegm, sneezing repeatedly, breathing heavily with a whistling noise, gasping, scratching, pulling at your crotch area, eating parts of you in any way, is not acceptable. They are considered extremely bad habits and an experience, mature individual who is going to be paid to represent the company, must not show any of these bad habits in public.

If you have any of these bad habits, now's the time to start working on them. The quickest way to make yourself more aware of unconscious habits with your hands is to wear gloves at home. Wear them for a few weeks to help break all habits (washing them daily, of course!)

Project that you're management material

You may not realize it, but some jobs asking for an entry level or junior worker, are actually designed to find a manager. I've known many people who've gone for what they thought was going to be an easy job and ended up supervising a store or office within a few months, purely because they had the skills, and no one else in the company was up to the manager's standards!

If you walk into the interview displaying management potential, it may also help you not only get that job, but get a promotion after six months too!

If you plan to work in an office and make a career of it, eventually you should be a supervisor, then manager, if not on the board of directors. Maybe that'll happen in two years, five years or longer, depending on what you want to do and where you are working.

These are the things you need to show you have, before you become a manager. To get that manager job in five years' time, you need to start acting like a manager today. Even in the first interview.

What do you need to have to be a good manager?

Charisma
Your personality and your ability to relate to everyone in the workplace, as well as your ability to influence other people, plays a very important role in your management of people.

Fairness
You should always show you treat everyone equally. If someone does something well you should reward them. If someone does something that is not good for the company, you should penalize them. These awards and punishments should be seen to be fair in the eyes of all your staff members.

Ability to listen and give credit
If you show you care about people's opinions you're more likely to be seen as a good manager of people and people are more likely to respect you.

Integrity
You must be seen as honest and trustworthy in the business environment. The best managers are believable and say it like it is. They're someone that staff can always rely on to help them with their job and represent the company's best interests. Someone with integrity continues to do the right thing when no one is looking and when no one would ever know.

Social understanding
When interviewing new staff, you should consider a person's personality on top of their skills, and make sure that that personality is compatible with the culture of your business environment. There's no point inviting someone to join a business if they're a hot-head only interested in money. Everyone should be able to enjoy working together.

Respect for staff

You should fight for your staff and work hard to get them business and keep them on. If you did a good job when interviewing them then you'll know every staff member is an asset and you will do everything in your power to give them a good working environment.

Forward Planning Abilities

Ability to plan ahead five to ten years, perhaps longer. Good managers are strategic planners and have vision and drive to plan for the long term.

So, if you can give the interviewer an idea that you might have management potential, he or she may consider you for a better role than the one you have applied for.

Avoid Direct Language

Now, being direct, using swear words and slang, and making rude jokes might be okay with your friends and on your social media accounts, but it is a bad idea in a job interview. Do you use direct language? Do you say things like 'Why?' instead of, 'I'm sorry, I hope you don't mind me asking, but could you tell me why we have to do that?' In an interview situation, you must do your absolute best to not be confrontational. If you do end up accidentally using a confrontational sentence, end with a smile and a laugh to indicate you're not trying to be offensive.

Here are some simple polite expressions. Do you use any of these? If you're always using polite expressions these would be part of your regular conversation. If you use none of these, then you'll need to look up polite expressions and integrate some into your normal day to day speaking habits, they'll then come through automatically in your interview.

Perhaps we should...
I'm not sure if...
Wouldn't it be better if...
There seems to be a mistake with...
I'm afraid that...
Is it alright if I...
Do you need any help with...
Would it be possible for you to...
To be honest, I'm not sure that...
Would you like to...
It might be a bit too...
I was wondering if you could...

Could you possibly…
It seems we have a slight problem with…

Fear of Embarrassing Situations

Many suffer from a fear of embarrassing situations. There is nothing much you can do about this, unfortunately. The longer you live, the more embarrassing situations you'll have. Contrary to belief, every single person in the world suffers embarrassing situations regularly. It's part of being human! It's best just to shake your head, laugh and move on.

There are three main types of embarrassing situations.

1. Saying the wrong thing.
2. Tripping, falling or walking into something.
3. Being one hundred percent positive about something, then being proven one hundred percent wrong.

How to avoid these embarrassing situations.
Apart from never putting yourself in these situations in the first place, there are three things you can do to improve your chances of avoiding an embarrassing situation.

Firstly, be very aware of your environment and consider everything you're about to say before you say it. There's no need to comment on someone's suspected pregnancy, for example (she might not be pregnant!) You can avoid most embarrassing slips of the tongue by listening carefully to everything that is being said around you.

Secondly, be extra careful of where you're walking. If you're going to speak with someone it's better to do it while standing still, not as you're heading out the door. Accidents do happen!

Thirdly, don't talk about topics unless you are sure of your facts, then refer to those facts. If it's a discussion where you are learning something new, that's fine. If you're trying to convert everyone around you to your point of view, be very sure to mention specific reports proving your point.

How to deal with an embarrassing situation once it happens
This is hard for most people but the main thing is to not make a big deal of it. Do your best to turn it into a joke.

If you say something stupid, say "Why did I say that? Someone must have put drugs in my coffee this morning." If you say something quickly to clear the air then move on, it won't be noticed as much and it will no longer be an embarrassing situation. If it is something barely anybody noticed, you can pretend nothing happened and keep going. This is what most newsreaders do when they read something incorrectly!

If you walk into something, you can say 'oh, who put that there,' and laugh.

If you find out something you've been telling everyone about is wrong, you can actually make a big deal of it like 'Oh My God I was so wrong. I can't believe it. Sooo embarrassing. I'm so sorry about that. Here is the correct information. Can you believe it?!' and laugh!

Embarrassing moments are moments in time. Best to laugh at them and move on. Most embarrassing moments are quickly forgotten. Just don't put them on YouTube!

Upgrade Your Vocabulary

Depending on the sort of job you are going for will depend on the kind of vocabulary you will need. Each industry has its own industry specific vocabulary. If you are experienced in this area, you'll be able to use the appropriate language in the interview. Managers will be listening to what you say that is relevant to the job.

If you're going for a general office job and the manager asks you specific questions about financial or business oriented subjects, you might want to know some more common business buzz words. I'd advise that you research these in your own time, and practice including them in your business conversations.

Business Buzz Words
Instead of saying 'releasing staff from their work contracts' you could say 'performing a head-count reduction.' Instead of saying 'problem' you could say 'challenge' or 'opportunity.' There are thousands of these words, and when you begin working in someone else's business you'll start hearing them almost immediately. Here are some to look out for. What do you think they mean?

achieve clarity
actualize
address the issue
backward-compatible

benchmarking
blamestorming
bleeding edge
bucketize
cash neutral
client focused
cloud (v.)
core competencies
ecosystem
holistic approach
incentivize
involuntary retirement
key player
leverage (v.)
mindshare
monetize
networking
offline (v.)
operationalize
optimization
paradigm shift
percolate
proactive
quality vector
repurpose
resource constrained
rubber stamp (verb)
solutions-oriented
synergize
touch base
traction
user-centric
value-added
vertical

One thing you may have noticed is that many business buzzwords are simply nouns converted to verbs. For example: "We need to table this now before we rubber stamp the project and incentivize the staff, otherwise we'll have to offline it for tomorrow."

New business buzzwords are invented every month and ones disappear as the industry that uses them becomes obsolete. You'll find hundreds of sites online with business buzzwords. It's highly recommended that if you plan to work in a business oriented office, you learn ten new buzzwords every day.

Social Networking – 'Be Awesome!'

You need your social networks buzzing about you. It doesn't mean you spam your friends, but it does mean you need to show you're an influencer or, at the very least, a go-to person for advice. All businesses will search your social media accounts to find out what you're like, without exception. Make sure all your posts are fun and interesting, and they'll be more interested in interviewing you.

Please don't confuse social networking with job networking. They're completely different. Job networking requires you to spam people you don't know to create a names list that you can then spam again to find a job. I do not recommend it.

Instead, create a social network of friends and family that love you, your tribe, and want to help you and they will give you some guidance on how you can find a job. And perhaps, one day, one of them might be running a business and offer you a job because they love you so much. That's another reason to be awesome on your social media accounts!

Some accounts employers will search if they're interested in you:

Facebook
Instagram
LinkedIn
SnapChat
Youtube
Twitter

If you want them to think that you are modern, up-to-date and able to deal with technology, then having these profiles online is mandatory. Every office worker has one. Many offices now have Office Facebook, so you need to be familiar with personal Facebook before you can use the Office one. If you don't have any of these, it would be like saying that you don't have email.

In 2012, I was teaching a TEFL course and discovered that one of the students who had joined the class to learn how to be a teacher had never ever used email and didn't know much about computers. He was in his thirties. I politely told him that he hadn't a chance in hell of getting a job as a teacher if he didn't know the absolute basics of what was required in the world these days, and that I had been using email since 1991, and uploading blogs, websites and online video productions since 1996, and doing SEO since 2000. I couldn't believe he'd missed over twenty years of human advancement.

Social media skills are mandatory. Even politicians have them. If you don't know, get someone to show you, asap. Though, if you didn't, I guess you probably wouldn't have found this eBook!

Some more searches businesses will do on you
• Search your cell number and email address via Google to see what ads you've posted.
• Search your name in quotes to see if you have any blogs.
• Search for your picture (!)
• Search for any videos you may have posted on Youtube, as well as the videos you've previously clicked 'like' on
• Search for details of your life, your relationships, your actions, your previous jobs, the sort of comments you make on forums, and much more.

If you have a great authentic internet presence, showing your honesty, integrity and your do-good nature, then you won't mind this intrusion into your privacy. After all, by it being online, you've already agreed to everything about yourself being public knowledge.

If you're concerned about privacy, this may not be something you would like to happen. In which case, you need to login to everything and set your privacy to high. It will mean people won't be able to request friendships on Facebook, or read your profile on LinkedIn. They would also have to send a personal request on Instagram, but you might wish to do it if you don't want a potential employer seeing pictures of your drunken weekend or your multiple girlfriends/boyfriends' pics.

You'll also need to visit places like Gumtree and Craigslist to remove your advertisements, as your ads can remain indexed on Google for years.

Using social media can be a double-edged sword. If you've only ever posted good things about yourself, then you can happily include your social media profile links in your resume too! If you have a negative, toxic social media presence with trolling and lots of rants about the world, you probably won't be considered for an interview.

Time to add some more points!

Updated your body language? 50 points
Can mirror people? 50 points

Got rid of other bad habits? 50 points
Projecting that you're management material? 50 points
Using polite language? 50 points
Improved your ability to deal with embarrassing situations? 50 points
Upgraded your vocabulary with some business buzzwords? 50 points
Set up some social network pages? 50 points for each one

[Trumpets]

Congratulations.

You've made it to Level 8.

You're now ready to go to an interview.

Level Up.

+10,000 points.

Level 8:
The Interviews

You're now ready to attend that interview. With everything you've done so far, you're probably ready to walk into that first interview and get offered a job on the spot.

But, just in case you haven't been to an interview before, what can you expect?

After your phone interview, there'll be a period of time (usually no more than two weeks) where your interview is considered (perhaps a recording of your answers is reviewed by a board) and your details are shuffled about in a folder of resumes. If you make it to the short list, you'll be called/emailed again.

To make your best impression with the company, especially if you are one of many candidates, you should be available for an interview at any time.

Yes, you can!
"Can you come for an interview at our rural location at 2am early morning? I know it's a four-hour drive in the middle of the night."
"Yes, of course I can!"

"Can you come for an interview at our desert office around 8pm? I realize it'll be about fifty degrees on that day but that's the best time for the boss."
"Yes, of course I can!"

"The boss is on the side of Mount Everest at the moment but he really wants to meet you. Can you fly there today?"
"Yes, of course I can!"

You get the idea. They'll be testing you to see if you really want the job. If you're "oh, my mum's coming to visit, I've got to take my friend to the airport, I'm still working at my other job, I'm sick, my father is dying in the hospital," then you're not who they're looking for. Just remember that, as much as society doesn't want us to think it, you must choose your job over your life if you want to be successful.

Skyping
These days, interviews in person are less common. It's much more likely you'll be doing Skype interviews. If this is the case, make sure your Skype software is up-to-date, that you're on a fast connection, and that you have professional headphones and microphone connected, tested and working.

You must also make sure that there aren't any programs connecting to the net to download updates while your Skype interview is working. If you're familiar with computers, I recommend installing a free program for windows called TinyWall which can even block unexpected Windows Updates! (Only do this if you know what you're doing.

As Skype interviews are somewhere between a phone interview and an in-person interview, I won't need to say much more on them. Learn from the phone interview information and the in-person interview information, then use that in your Skype interviews.

Finally!
So, the interview is booked and it is a time that is convenient to the business, and it is on a day that they're seeing many other candidates.

You've read the dialogue above with the nervous person in the waiting room. Don't be that person. Arrive about five minutes before the interview (wait somewhere else in the suburb if you arrive early, don't wait on the premises. Don't show that you're too eager, but don't be late either.)

Be on time
If something has happened that there was no way you could anticipate, like a fire in your apartment building or a six train pile up at a railway intersection, then you can ring and advise how sorry you are and that you'll be a few minutes late.

If it is something you can avoid, like a late bus (buses are always late) a traffic jam on the highway (there are always traffic jams on highways) then you don't have an excuse as you could simply have left your home earlier to be there on time. I had a girl turn up for a meeting half an hour late, no apology, and then when I ask why she was late she simply said 'Oh, my bus was late, nothing I could do,' like it wasn't important. That was at least $30 lost productivity using my time because she didn't make the effort to plan ahead.

No common sense, no job!

Make sure you plan ahead so well that nothing will stop you from getting there on time.

What to bring

Bring a printed version of your resume, a copy of the ad to keep reminding you why you're there, and any other material you think might be relevant. If it is a design job you'll probably bring a printed portfolio of your best work.

Of course, these items are rarely looked at as you would have sent digital copies already, but there are some employers that are so rushed, and can't find your resume, or their computer crashes when they're about to check it, and they'd be grateful that you have a copy to give them. You can also leave a copy anyway at the end, if you think that the interview went well – an extra reminder to get them thinking about you.

Personal Story
When I went for my first interview at a bookshop, I brought along some books I'd written myself on my old typewriter. Typed them up, cut up the pages, put them into bound formats. I wanted to show how much I loved books.

When I went for an SEO consultancy job I brought along my netbook with screen grabs of Alta Vista and Yahoo screen results showing how I'd got many of my sites into the top ten (this was BG: Before Google)

If there is something in addition to what is needed you think might be useful in getting the position, bring it along. Even if you sent them a link to your online portfolio before, it's possible that the person who is about to interview you hasn't had time to see it yet. You may find it useful to mention it.

The First In-Person Interview

The receptionist/personal assistant/secretary will call people in, one by one. Note the people who are there when you arrive and see which ones leave before you. Some may arrive late but still go in before you, depending on the time that is scheduled. If all the people who were there before you have already been to the interview, you're probably up next!

Lots of possibilities may happen next. The receptionist may ask you to follow them and they will take you in and introduce you to the person who will interview you, or they may tell you the location and you have to find your way there yourself.

You might find the door closed or open. If the door has only recently closed, then it is okay to simply open it again and walk in confidently. If the door has been closed for a while, it might be best to knock.

If you're going through an agency, you might be in an open plan office with other agents interviewing other people around you.

Or the agent may take you to a meeting room nearby.

If you are being interviewed by an agent, they will do their best to find you a job as it will be in their best interests. They'll get a commission. Make sure you're a product that they want to sell.

Or you might be part of a group of a hundred people all being lectured about a standard marketing job, what's required, and then a handful are left as some take their leave, deciding it's not worth their time. (Think clipboard charity funds sourcing on street corners!)

Many interviews are not in offices. It's possible the interviewer will take you to a local café to be interviewed. He/she will meet you at reception and offer to buy you tea or coffee. It's good form to say 'oh, I'd be happy to pay,' but if this is your hundredth interview, you may decide to go with the free drink. Don't say 'I don't like tea or coffee' as you'd already be making the manager feel uncomfortable, and making him/her think that if the interview hasn't even started yet and you're already wanting to change things for yourself, you're going to be too much of a handful in the office. Even if you don't like tea or coffee, go with it. It can still sit there on the table, and you don't need to drink it all. Just a sip and focus on the interview.

You'll be guided to a seat, and your interviewer will begin with some chitchat, depending on where you live. In the UK or Australia, it might be about the weather, the traffic or a recent sports game. Go with whatever chit chat is appropriate. Generally, you'll end up agreeing with the interviewer.

Depending on the interviewer, they may start asking you questions immediately, or they will launch into what their company does and what kind of employee they're looking for. They'll subtly observe your expression as they go through the points. (We realize you've probably forgotten everything in the ad by the time you've taken a seat, so we usually go over it again, depending on the position.)

After the interviewer is sure you understand everything about the job and what is expected, they'll start with some basic questions about you, moving through questions about your performance then finish with questions about future goals and career aspirations. Or, maybe they'll mix things up just to keep you on your toes!

The interview then concludes with them asking if you have any questions. If you have been listening closely, you should have some questions about the job.

Questions to avoid in the first interview (unless you are going through an agent)

How much will I earn?

Is there time and a half and double time on weekends?

How many sick days will I get?

What's your superannuation plan?

How much is the tax?

Do you offer a commission on sales?

What are my working hours?

If your goal is to get a job, any kind of job, then you won't need to focus on money in the first interview. If your goal is to get a much better job than the one you already have, then you should already know the amount that is being offered before you even apply for the interview. Either way, discussing your personal benefits at the end of the interview, before you're even moved to a short list, means that your focus is just getting money to survive, not helping the business, and so you will be less likely to make it to the next interview. Save those questions for the final interview.

Because, yes, there'll be another interview!

The Second In-Person Interview

If there are a lot of candidates, it is likely you'll be called back for a second, more stressful interview. This will involve a number of important people who will interrogate you – quick staccato questions from three different managers that may leave you feeling very nervous. Keep your cool and don't let it get to you. You're going to get a lot of pressure in the job so if you're not up to the pressure of that kind of interview, you're unlikely to be suitable for the job anyway.

Unlikely to be much chitchat, barely any questions about your character, lots of questions about your performance. Prepare yourself for questions about failures in previous jobs or life situations, how you dealt with them, how you made money for other businesses and more.

You're also likely to have your skills tested. In the first interview, you may be asked to do a simple touch-typing or math test. In this interview, you're likely to be using a dummy version of the software program required for your job. Depending on your behavior in the interview and your performance on the software, you may get the job, or if they still can't decide, you might be called back for a third interview.

The Third In-Person Interview

For entry level and non-supervisor/manager positions it is unlikely you'll be called back for a third interview. For management positions, interviews could be ongoing. If you're applying for a CEO position you may have to do multiple interviews with a variety of stakeholders around the world, with the interview process lasting months to years.

If you do get that third interview, it means you're so close to getting that job you can feel it. It's possible that there are just two candidates for the position left and you need to pull out all the stops to get that position. At this point the possibilities are endless as to what you can do, and if you get to this stage, I can only wish you the best of luck! What you have learnt by this point will have given you the edge on everyone else and only you will know the best way to proceed from this point.

At absolutely any point in these interview processes you could be offered the job. Sometimes you get lucky and there just aren't enough people applying, or there aren't enough people with the skills they're looking for that you have. Sometimes you get the job at the end of the interview when they say 'Well, I'm happy with what I've heard today, so you've got the job. When you can you start?'

Sometimes they are waiting for you to ask for the job. If you thought the interview went well, it's your turn to say. "Well, what do you think? Can I have the job? I'm happy to start work whenever you need me!" If they have been really impressed with you already, it's possible they'll say yes and move directly to giving you forms to fill out. This can be quite a shock, but it does happen.

Sometimes the review process is long and tiring and, just when you think you may have got it, they call you in to meet a new manager to go through the process again because the person that interviewed you before was fired! Or in the case of a government position, there's been an election and things have changed so the job position has disappeared. Or the company has closed. Or the CEO has decided to move the company interstate. Or…

Anything can happen even in the interview process. Even at the point when they offer the job to you. Even in the first week of working.

One of my students went for a job and got it immediately. Then spent two weeks waiting for the person who was in the position he had been hired to take over, to leave. There was a delay with the project and that person couldn't leave, so my friend waited another four weeks doing nothing in the job, wondering if he really had the job, and then the person left and he could finally work.

This is why, even after you have confirmed lots of interviews, you should continue with your resume and cover letter posting. You have no idea what can happen, even after being in the job for four weeks. And, who knows, you may get a better offer and quit the job you just got!

Didn't get the job?

You still got some training! What could you have done better?

Sometimes, it's just bad luck that you didn't get the job. There was someone better skilled, living closer, fitter, healthier, smarter, more connected, more experienced, more trained etc. etc. that applied at the same time as you. It happens all the time, and the best thing is to just stay positive and try again.

Additional Tips

Here are some additional tips that may or may not apply to you. If you've been going to interviews for weeks and still can't get success, try doing some of these things.
• Update your voicemail to be professional.
• Create an email address that is professional sounding. (You know, adding one of those automatic signatures that say 'Private and Confidential. If you have received this email incorrectly please… etc. etc.)
• Update your skills in whatever software the job you're applying for may be using.
• Improve your English skills in speaking and writing. Enunciation, clear speaking. Get a pronunciation tutor.
• Practice interviews with your friends.
• Record yourself on video in a mock interview situation and get people to point things out. Slouching in the chair? Laughing too hard? Not looking people in the eye? Sweating? Fix these simple things.

After you have done a few interviews you will have begun to create your own interview techniques - ways you do things that you find other people like. You will also have noticed things you do that they don't like, and changed these things in the interview process to make yourself more appealing.

Think of each interview as a training course and, as you get more experienced with them, you'll be able to breeze through them until that perfect job appears, and you won't need to do them again for a while!

Resources

If the job wasn't for you and there aren't that many out there, you might find this list of resources useful. Visit their websites or their apps via iTunes or Google Play to find and apply to more jobs, or to read further information on finding a job.

www.BeKnown.com
www.Craigslist.com
www.Ideal.com
www.JobAware.com
www.Jobcompass.com
www.LinkedIn.com
www.Linkup.com
www.Reach.com
www.SimplyHired.com
www.SnagAJob.com
www.Switch.com
www.ZipRecruiter

Other places to find a job
• Local Government/Community job organizations
• Direct to Agencies
• Teachers at schools and universities
• Military organizations
• Job support groups
• Door knocking, letter box drops,
• Volunteering

Places to advertise yourself simply
Google AdWords
Bing Ads
YouTube Video
Twitter Ads
Facebook Ads
LinkedIn Ads

And many other places to advertise online, if you have the advertising budget to spend. Think a minimum spend per ad $100, with clicks starting from $2.

Can't find any job you would like to do, but still like the idea of an office?

Then you, my friend, have the opportunity to get a few people together and start your own business.

Degrees didn't exist before the 14th century and offices didn't exist before the 17th century. These are modern inventions. For thousands of years, humanity survived by running their own businesses on what they knew. Either it was passed down to them, or they got an apprenticeship somewhere and learnt it themselves. Whether that was something simple like fixing shoes or making swords, or something more complicated like designing chain mail armor for the king, or creating new types of drinks, we did our own thing.

If you have a passion to do something different, you'll find a way and the people to help you. Find a way to avoid the whole office game.

Want to do something in between, like work for yourself, but doing freelance work? Try

www.UpWork.com
www.Fiverr.com
www.Freelancer.com
www.AirTasker.com

Were you tempted to drop the whole office job idea?

No? Not ready to give up yet? Good! Keep trying!

If you have completed all the exercises, and worked above and beyond what is expected, you have probably made it past 12,000 points. Well done!

Keep working on sending those resumes and cover letters. That job is so close you can probably smell it! Keep at it. Don't lose momentum!

Got the job? Congratulations! You are now

'Proficient'

Advanced Level

But, it's not over yet!

Now that you've got the job, you've got to keep it!

Add 20,000 points and level up

Level 9: Keeping a Job

It's fantastic that you have been able to get a job. That's great news. Now you must keep it.

Everything you were taught in this book, everything you've learnt from other sources, everything you did and promised in the interview, you now need to show in your job.

Make sure you work hard, learn quickly, and make yourself as indispensable to the business as possible in the shortest period of time. You don't want anyone thinking they may have made a mistake by hiring you.

Many businesses have a minimum three months' trial period. Some have six, some have twelve. Make sure you know what your trial period length is. They can fire you at any time without notice during this period, so you should still be sending out your resumes and cover letters if you think that you may not be in the job for long.

When you reach six months+ in the job, and they confirm that you are now a permanent employee, you have reached the level of expert.

Congratulations, expert office worker.

You have won the game.

Well done.

Bonus 50,000 points

So, what's next?

Been in the job for at least two years?

Reached the limit of what you can achieve there?

It's time to…

Play again!

Final Note from Jason

Thank you for reading this title. I hope you have found it useful.

If you followed everything in this book and got a job, please post your review on your favorite platform. I'd love to hear your success story.

If you followed everything, but still couldn't get a job, please post your review letting me know what you think might be missing from this eBook. It will mean I can make the next edition better.

Wishing you all the best in your job hunting.

Cheers

Jason

P.S. I mainly now work as a private English tutor, author, and voice actor, but I am occasionally available for job coaching via Skype. If you'd like to hire me for a one-hour interview practice, visit my website at www.EziEnglish.com to find out more.

Other Titles From Maldek House

Written by
Jason Hogan

IELTS Speaking Practice Tests

ESL Dialogues and Conversations Scripts

Edited by
Jason Hogan

IELTS General Training Reading Practice Tests

IELTS Academic Training Reading Practice Tests

Find out more at

www.EziEnglish.com

Weekly Planner Diary
52 Blank Undated Weeks
Lined Note Pages &
Century Planner
Find out more on Amazon
If you prefer a printed diary rather than a digital one...